1 MONTH OF
FREE
READING

at
www.ForgottenBooks.com

By purchasing this book you are eligible for one month membership to ForgottenBooks.com, giving you unlimited access to our entire collection of over 1,000,000 titles via our web site and mobile apps.

To claim your free month visit:
www.forgottenbooks.com/free206890

* Offer is valid for 45 days from date of purchase. Terms and conditions apply.

ISBN 978-0-266-21389-5
PIBN 10206890

This book is a reproduction of an important historical work. Forgotten Books uses state-of-the-art technology to digitally reconstruct the work, preserving the original format whilst repairing imperfections present in the aged copy. In rare cases, an imperfection in the original, such as a blemish or missing page, may be replicated in our edition. We do, however, repair the vast majority of imperfections successfully; any imperfections that remain are intentionally left to preserve the state of such historical works.

Forgotten Books is a registered trademark of FB &c Ltd.
Copyright © 2018 FB &c Ltd.
FB &c Ltd, Dalton House, 60 Windsor Avenue, London, SW19 2RR.
Company number 08720141. Registered in England and Wales.

For support please visit www.forgottenbooks.com

aw- ewar

by
Ronald Knox

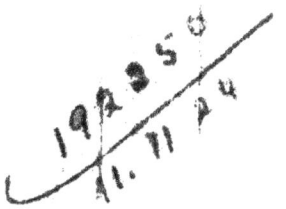

PALL MALL, S.W.
WILLIAM COLLINS SONS & CO. LTD.
GLASGOW MELBOURNE AUCKLAND
1920

Patrick Shaw-Stewart

by Ronald Knox

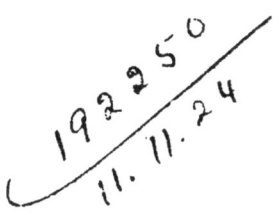

48 PALL MALL, S.W.
WILLIAM COLLINS SONS & CO. LTD.
GLASGOW MELBOURNE AUCKLAND
1920

Chapter One

IT may be easily thought that the times are too late for War biographies. While the public felt it almost heartless to indulge in any other literature than that bearing on the one subject which prepossessed it, the demand for such biographies was natural. Now that the spectre has passed by, do we do well to linger still over the details of individual lives cut short, instead of burying the very memories of our dead in a cenotaph of common fame? There is more public appetite, perhaps, for Post-War revelations, for the bandying of 'I told you so' and 'Your fault all the time' between public and ex-public characters. But it is to be hoped that there are some who are inclined to tend the ashes of memory in a more generous spirit, and to pause a moment longer before they turn away from the imperfect monuments of a generation that died before its time.

They utter no I-told-you-so's, those patient rivals of living greatness, they do not impute fault. They have left to others the two-volume biographies, with index and map. Few of them had the opportunity to play a part which in itself made a story worth the telling. Their letters do not speak of advances or of hand-to-hand fighting, but of books, of quiet hours, of welcome rest-camps; they appeal, not for credit or for sympathy, but for trivial daily needs,

Patrick Shaw-Stewart.

pathetic because trivial—boot-polish and pipe-cleaners and shaving soap. Tight corners there were, and hair-breadth escapes, but they did not mention these—did not mention them at least in letters home, or to those who, in reading such accounts, might feel their hearts quicken at the reading. There is a great deal of sameness in the experiences, and one soldier's letter might easily stand for another. Is it necessary, then, that they should all lie under a common mound of earth, *indiscretum atque immiserabile vulgus*? To be sure, that honourable sepulture is enough record of their deaths. But if some more than others laid down lives rich in promise, flowers without fruit, yet already marked out by some earnest of their futuribles; if some more than others had the eye which sees the significant or the picturesque detail, and the pen in some measure trained to record it, need the survivors, the two-volume men, be jealous if we try to preserve a few phrases of such authorship, a few living echoes of what they felt, or rather —for their letters always cheated us just a little— of what they meant us to think they were feeling?

If any such distinctions are to be drawn, if we can contrive to make some memories vocal without slighting those other memories that are dumb, it needs no further preface or apology to give Patrick Shaw-Stewart a memoir of his own. The many friends who mourn him will feel that something is lacking to the Epic cycle which includes the *aristeia* of Charles Lister and the Grenfells, if the

Patrick Shaw-Stewart.

tale stops short at Τάφον Ἕκτορος. And a larger public, when it reads of an Eton and Balliol scholar, winner of the Newcastle, the Ireland, and so many other academic laurels, a fellow of All Souls', who could transfer himself lightly (though none of us supposed finally) to finance, and hold the position of a Managing Director in Baring Brothers before he had reached twenty-five, may guess that this was not one of the passengers of his generation.

Yet all who knew him will realise the difficulty of making such a record. His penetrating insight and his perfect humour played for preference always with people, not with things, and a good part of his letters, if it were published so as to be understood, would have to be accompanied with a whole Targum of footnotes, of intolerable dreariness. Of literary remains he himself regrets, as will be seen, that he has left practically nothing. When he was called upon to write (for example) a paper for a society at Oxford, he would always put off the evil day till the last moment, and dash off what was in the circumstances a brilliant performance without leaving anything for posterity to cherish. He had a genius for relating means to ends, for doing just so much work as was required to gain this scholarship, for making just so much impression as was required to consolidate this acquaintanceship; and his whole life (I think) was mapped out on a plan which involved the acquisition of an assured position in the world before he began to toy with literature,

Patrick Shaw-Stewart.
with Movements, with serious politics. This plan, in itself so admirable, so much to be recommended to the many whose desire for self-expression leads them to express themselves far too early, is all lamentable to the biographer. There are only two sections in this book which were even remotely designed by him for publication—his account, written from Salonica, of his own school days, and his description of the *Hood* Battalion's Argo-voyage, which was meant to be a contribution to the memoir of Charles Lister.

Further, he acquired at Eton the habit of writing in a sort of parody of journalese. The parody was perfectly conscious; he never thought that he was writing good English when he used long words and far-fetched adjectival periphrases. I must implore every reader of this book to remember that whenever Patrick wrote, he wrote (as we used to say) 'in inverted commas': it was not the style but the parody of a style which was intended to catch your fancy. I do not mean that he copied journalists' phrases; I mean that he wrote as a journalist would write who possessed, and knew that his readers possessed, a very complete classical education, an almost verbatim knowledge of the Bible, and an intimate acquaintance with certain periods of history and literature; in the spirit of such an imaginary character he coined language for himself instead of facing—when had he the time for it?—the scholar's task of making language do justice to his thought.

Patrick Shaw-Stewart.

But it was not only his style that was in inverted commas; he was perpetually in inverted commas to himself. I do not mean merely that he had the very rare gift of seeing a joke against himself and could enjoy, for all his Scottish proper pride, the memory of an occasion when he had cut a ridiculous figure: it went far deeper than that. He had in boyhood—I do not hesitate to record the fact, although I have not included in this book the documentary evidence which supports it—a quality which he calls 'hypertrophy of conscience,' what is technically known as 'scrupulosity.' The fear that he had done less than justice to his prayers, or that he had taken unfair advantage of a rival, used to weigh on his spirits like a nightmare. He outlived these particular symptoms, but it is not difficult to trace in them the parentage of that fierce candour both about himself and about other people which sometimes left his friends aghast. He hated false enthusiasms and sham certainties; an enthymeme, for him, should never do duty for a syllogism. He could not bear that any action of his should be ascribed to a good motive if there were any unworthy motive that had put a grain on the balance of decision. I have known him refuse a slight proffered benefit with, 'Now, then, none of your damned Christian charity.' All this means that whatever you find him saying about himself must be treated as evidence for the prosecution, not for the defence. He did not make truth an idol, but he had almost a mania for candour.

Patrick Shaw-Stewart.

The letters which have been used in the compilation of this book were mostly family letters, supplied by his two sisters and his old nurse. For this reason (since superscriptions and valedictions are apt to become wearisome where there is no great variety of correspondents) I have given extracts from letters as a rule in preference to complete letters, and have not been careful to distinguish in all cases the name of the addressee, though I hope I have left enough character in the selection of what he wrote to his nurse ' Dear ' to illustrate something of his constant affection and thoughtfulness for her. Having so many family letters before me, I have naturally refused to go on the principle that nothing written before the War can have its biographical interest. On the contrary, it seems probable that whereas the War period will be easy for the historians of the future to reconstruct, their difficulty will be to catch the atmosphere of those halcyon 1913 days, when we lived so carelessly and so vigorously, before we had learned to kill all generous effort by labelling it ' Reconstruction.' Personality does not spring into being with an identity disc.

I must, however, record my gratitude to others who have been kind enough to supply me with material from the letters they had preserved, especially Lady Desborough, Lady Horner, Mrs Raymond Asquith, and Lady Hermione Buxton. In arranging the extracts, I have tried to obtrude as little as possible in the way of comment or reflection, leaving the reader to isolate, to admire,

Patrick Shaw-Stewart.

and to skip what he chooses. Where I have commented at any length, it is only because, as I have indicated above, it was Patrick's way to try and make us all think the worst of him, and the interests of the very candour which he insisted upon demand that, in some points, the impression made should be supplemented by the more sparing criticism of an impartial witness.

Chapter Two

PATRICK HOUSTON SHAW-STEWART was born on the 17th of August, 1888, the son of Major-General John Heron Maxwell Shaw-Stewart, and Mary Catherine Bedingfeld, only child of Colonel George Chancellor Collyer. His Scottish origin, his membership of a military family, and the fact that his elder brother Basil was considerably older than himself, should account for a certain reverence for his elders as such, which was native to him—he was one of the few people in his generation to whom it came natural to address men considerably older than himself as ' Sir.' This was part of a general Toryism of outlook; he was an unabashed Conservative in politics, an ardent defender of sport and of the military virtues, and had a solid respect for the conventions of an ordered society. In keeping with such traditions, he had a habit of personal self-respect which it was easy to recognise in spite of that absence in him of tidiness and punctuality which often goes with first-class brains. This conventional background, not wholly in harmony with the traditions of the generation into which he was born, or of the society in which he afterwards figured, was permanent with him, and may be laid down as the preface to his development.

There are a few early letters, which show some marks of precocity. The date (August, 1895) lends

Patrick Shaw-Stewart.

interest to the statement, ' I have discovered out of Grandfather's GEOLOGY book, that MAN is nothing but a highly developed ANTHROPOID APE (*Simius Homo Sapiens*).' And there is an early trace of the determination not to be carried away by merely conventional enthusiasms in a letter which belongs to the following month : ' We went to Keswick and Derwentwater on the 18th. We had a perfectly lovely day. We got there at 2 p.m., and after about three-quarters of an hour waiting, went on to Lodore,

> See how the water
> Goes down at Lodore—

Indeed it would have been quite true, if there had only been some more water.' But for precocious comment on life we should go to a letter written some time later, in February, 1902, after he had been a half at Eton (he is referring to a lady who showed him round a picture-gallery), ' This she accomplished very creditably, I think—she took us most manfully round all the pictures in the galleries and talked sufficiently the while (of all offences I cannot stand a dumb girl!) ' A rapidly developed fondness for long words is noticeable, even before he goes to Eton :—

' The atmosphere here is not exactly conducive to a superabundant flow of correspondence, so this small effusion must, I am afraid, content the

Patrick Shaw-Stewart.
inmates of No. 7 for a long, long time.—As I wrote to Father, time now seems to pass in one delicious, lingering dream of four meals a day and then bed, with occasionally more exciting work interspersed, such as the record number of eggs this year—24—which I managed to discover yesterday.

' I have at last found my métier—my real occupation in life; in fact the only useful thing I can do here, and which I much prefer to gardening, and all the other occupations—that is chopping up wood.

' I feel like George Washington or Mr Gladstone, and you have such a good and comfortable feeling when you see your own handiwork blazing on the " ospitable 'earth." ' [APRIL 12, 1901.]

But few boys come to their own at all till they reach a public school, and this is probably the more true in Patrick's case since he was never at a boarding school until he got a scholarship at Eton and came to College in the autumn of 1901. He seems to have felt this himself, for the description he himself wrote of his Eton school-time was apparently meant to be the first chapter in a sort of autobiography he had planned. This and an account of his time at Balliol were both written while he was on service at Salonica, but the latter document was somehow lost in transit, and, perhaps discouraged by this, he never went on with the project. The result is that we have a record of his early school sensations far completer than any we have of his

Patrick Shaw-Stewart.

later career; and it seems simplest to reproduce this at once in the place where he meant it to come. It is not easy to say whether he meant the document for publication as it stood; certainly he has taken the trouble to allude only distantly and by initials to the people who come into it. Probably he would have revised it; and, in uncertainty as to how drastic this revision would have been, I have gone on the principle of omitting those passages which might conceivably give pain to living persons, as well as those which deal with religion or with the higher emotions—a principle which, in the main, I have followed throughout the book. Opinions differ widely as to how much piety should withhold from the public view; in the long run, the editor has simply to fall back on his own feelings. I will only say that the revisions I have made reduce the document to about three-quarters of its original length, but, for the most part, they are not such as to interrupt the general course of the narrative.

' My first half was a welter of strange emotions, from which I emerged with a feeling of completeness and confidence which was yet to be shaken before it was established on a more cynical basis. In my first Christmas holidays I fell wholly back into family life (than which I as yet suspected nothing more satisfying) and correspondingly suffered from nostalgia on returning to Eton. In my second half I tended towards unhappiness, but was saved by a timely attack of chicken-pox which

Patrick Shaw-Stewart.
restored me for an extra month to the bosom of my family, followed by an extra long visit to beloved Findon. In a letter dated the beginning of the summer half next following this, I find myself saying, " The other boys all seem to have the centre of their life here, but I am still centred at home "—still the day-boy, still feminine influences, which were destined to disappear for four years, and then return. This summer half was marked by persistent failure at cricket, which I had mistakenly regarded as my game; from this moment I became embittered with it, and never again took it seriously—a grave disillusion in an athletic microcosm. After my first year at Eton my father took a small house near Inverness, where, for the moment, I was content in reunion, and remained free of aspiration towards such toys as guns and grouse. I stayed a week with Alan Parsons at Ballater, and he a week with me.

' My next year at Eton was perhaps my least happy : the extreme cosiness of " Chamber " life was forgone, my contemporaries were more impatient of my idiosyncrasies, and those idiosyncrasies had as yet shown no trace of modification; and, while making no further athletic progress, I was twice robbed of my very marked scholastic preëminence by Foss Prior and an oppidan (whom, indeed, he or I always beat, but who always added to the mortification of one of us by coming in an invariable second). I was at this time absolutely devoid of social prudence, a quality which suddenly

Patrick Shaw-Stewart.

developed itself in me at the turning point of my adolescence. As an instance, I clearly remember how easily I was persuaded to cox one of two Junior House Fours which College put on the river: a thankless office from every point of view, for it discredited me as even a humble dry-bob, classed me with a ridiculous set of little scugs and scamps, mocked me with an ephemeral cap only to be worn during the race itself, and provided in the actual exercise no opportunity whatever for distinction or applause, but a diversity of openings—of which I plentifully availed myself—for making myself look foolish.

' At about this period came a slight dissatisfaction with my holidays in London, later to spread to the summer in Scotland : though as eager as ever for the end of the half,* and still touched with homesickness, I now began to find the time hang heavy on me during the five weeks of family Christmas holiday. My second summer holidays near Inverness I remember to have been occupied with golf (Alan Parsons stayed with us again), and with the faint suggestion of feminine romance. Most important in this second year was a considerable intellectual quickening, which was perhaps stimulated by my two winter defeats in Trials, and which incidentally carried me to a sweeping victory in the summer. In the autumn I had the good fortune to be under the mellow influence of A. C. Benson, and in the summer I came into the hands of Hugh Macnaghten, not to emerge for a year. The former

Patrick Shaw-Stewart.

encouraged us to express ourselves in English, the latter opened the eyes of some of us to the true meaning of a classical education. Eton in my time certainly did offer opportunities to those who would avail themselves thereof, the greatest, perhaps, though unobtrusive and esoteric, being reserved for those who were under C. M. Wells in Head's Division. My third year was for the most part supremely uneventful. I performed the normal functions of adolescence such as going into tails, and (still unusual then) joining the Volunteers. I played for Lower College at football, and continued to be incompetent and unsuccessful at cricket. I remember opening the season with seven successive blobs in Junior Matches, till my nerve was reduced to pulp. At this time I made friends with ———, not a popular boy, perhaps a little *faute de mieux*; but, looking back, I think he was in his way excellent company and rather good for me. He taught me a little rather Ishmaelitish self-assurance, which at that time I sorely needed. (It is curious to remember the three boys who were at that time the undisputed social leaders of my election, and to ruminate on the benevolent feelings, tinged with anything rather than awe, with which I now regard them. Yet one of them at least had in a high degree the essential qualities of boy-leadership, and the other two at any rate a fine, early flowering sense of social values.) Academically this year was full of vicissitudes. At Christmas (1903) I repeated my summer's triumph in Trials

Patrick Shaw-Stewart.

and crowned it with a total of marks—1290 out of 1450—which must have come near making a record for these puerile and mechanical contests; and I had reason to hope (these intricacies are intelligible to Etonians alone) that the order I then established would be crystallised by our promotion into First Hundred. Actually, however, this was deferred for another half, at the end of which I was defeated by Foss Prior, our promotion was certain, and my chances of being Captain of the School seemed gone irretrievably. At that time the prospect of the Captaincy seemed to me my only chance of cutting a figure in the School.

'The next half (Summer, 1904), being disappointed of my great hope and at the same time promoted to First Hundred, I flung myself desperately into the work for the Certificate examination, became interested in the Colossians, and enamoured of the Seven Against Thebes, and to every one's astonishment carried off the Reynold's Scholarship, not only over the heads of the eminent seniors such as Daniel Macmillan, but also over Ronald Knox, one year senior to me, with whom I now crossed swords for the first time. This surprising success gave me great self-confidence and a considerable reputation for precocity.

'I returned to Eton in September, 1904, to begin my fourth year, notable in two of its halves for my very last sustained intellectual effort (with one transient exception) till after an interval of just four years. Athletically I was mildly pleased by having

Patrick' Shaw-Stewart.

my shorts as Junior Keeper of Lower College Game, but everything else, as Michaelmas Half gave way to Lent, faded before the really vigorous effort I proposed to make for the Newcastle, which had a peculiar significance in my mind. There was a tradition that the Newcastle Scholar, if not actually in Sixth Form at the time (I was in Second Division under the businesslike and excellent tuition of F. H. Rawlins), was promoted into it forthwith—this would in my case, of course, reverse my defeat by Foss Prior on promotion into First Hundred. To the workings of this tradition in my brain was joined the consciousness that it was possible for me to beat Ronald Knox. I girt myself accordingly to a terrific struggle against endless obscurity and the second place in the school, and quaintly enough I set about it. The Scriptural part of the examination was highly susceptible of preparation, the classical part—being an ordinary scholarship gamut—practically not at all; and yet I spent the best part of a valuable month in reading the *Birds* on a peculiar system of my own without notes or crib. In the same way afterwards I ploughed slowly and deliberately through the Scripture texts, always (from some confused conscientious scruple) reading every word of a book once begun, and—I am almost sure—refraining from marking down the side. I must have handicapped myself infinitely; and yet my memory and paper lucidity carried me through, and, defeated by Ronald Knox in Classics, I defeated him (the priest-to-be) sufficiently in Divinity to

Patrick Shaw-Stewart.

upset the balance and take the Scholarship. This, in the Eton world, was fame indeed. I was greatly petted and applauded, and tremendously happy.

'I returned for the Summer Half, and was promoted to Sixth Form *honoris causa*. I rejoiced in stick-up collars and a fag of my own; I shook off the spectre of Foss Prior's captaincy—and at that very moment began to wonder whether it really mattered so very much after all. At the time of which I am writing I still abounded in shynesses and gaucheries; I was still smiled at as an inept and academic Tug in Second Lower Club, and I remember being painfully conscious of a severe, patchy baldness (alopecia), which may or may not have been connected with my work for the Newcastle but which was certainly ill-timed to coincide with the bare-headed privileges of Sixth Form. At first I did not in the least realise—though no doubt my tutor did—the results that were certain to accrue from my premature successes in the Certificate and Newcastle. For the remaining two years and a half of my presumed Eton existence I had absolutely nothing to strive for, except the Balliol Scholarship, which, consisting of course entirely of " Scholarship papers," did not demand any very anxious preparation. Half consciously, therefore, I settled down to more than two years of complete idleness, for which there was this to be said, that it gave me the opportunity for self-realisation (as the authors say) in other spheres where previously I had genuinely circumscribed myself by the quite considerable

Patrick Shaw-Stewart.

assiduity of my work. I do not refer to athletics, because my development there, though its humble fruits date from this time, was perfectly normal, and I had never actually forgone a football after 4 to work—I think I only habitually stayed in after 4 in my Newcastle half, which was of course a Fives half—but rather to social intercourse and general reading. The last I still neglected after my Newcastle emancipation, as I neglected it again at Balliol and All Souls', and always till the City had engulfed me. For this I shall never forgive myself. Just before Lord's of this half (July, 1905), the abovementioned alopecia grew worse, and an eminent doctor ordered me to Switzerland, where I proceeded with my sister, and for a month danced about on the great Aletsch Glacier in the uncongenial company of about twenty parsons. Incidentally, I fear that I was very cross and selfish on this expedition, an impiety which I deeply regret, for I can never repay or deserve a tenth of the amazing affection always lavished on me by my sisters.

'In August we returned to Scotland, where my father had taken a new house near Tain. Here there was rough shooting, and I missed a great many rabbits and a few black game. I then went back to Eton (September, 1905), for a curious half which had on the whole a good bracing effect on me. I began by getting my College Wall sixth choice, which normally assured me my Mixed Wall unless College were beaten. Soon afterwards ——, who had left, came up for the day, and he and I, with

Patrick Shaw-Stewart.

two others, were found playing bridge in my room. Then came St Andrew's Day. The game was a draw: in the evening there was the Centenary Dinner of College Debating Society, and (feeling secure of my Mixed Wall) I got gloriously drunk on alternate glasses of hock and claret. (How pathetic it sounds! But it is strictly true.) My tutor discovered it, and I went before the head master, and was removed from Sixth Form for the rest of the half, as well as being compelled to take an informal pledge to cover the rest of my time at school. Back I went to low collars, and solitary at the end of the row in Chapel I awaited the Sixth Form procession. Two days later another got his Mixed Wall in my stead. A very depressed youth, I made my way to Balliol, where the cellar hospitality extended to all scholarship candidates was a mere mockery to the abstainer, and there did myself moderate justice with the third scholarship.

'Returning to Eton, I adorned myself with my forgone College Field, and ended the half comparatively a notability: a Balliol scholar elect, a two-colour man (alas! two colours seldom known apart to oppidans), and in the eyes of the small fry a great dare-devil. The next holidays and the following half were equally unimportant, placid, and vacuous. Of the holidays I remember nothing at all; of the half there is nothing to report. I was restored to my honours, and committed no new crimes. During this half I think I must have made rather closer acquaintance with prominent oppidans through

Patrick Shaw-Stewart.

Charles Lister and Ronald Knox, now both in Pop —probably with Edward Horner, certainly with Julian Grenfell. At the end I had full measure of the *suave mari magno* while others strove for the Newcastle. (I made a curious offer on the subject in connection with Ronald Knox's disability, quashed by the Provost.)[1]

'The summer half of 1906 was a great time for me from that purely snobbish point of view which is so vitally important to every boy in the last two years of school. It became charged for me with an added importance when George Fletcher decided to stay on till Christmas. I would therefore be second in the School after the summer, and instead of a safe election to Pop *ex officio*, I should either have a glorious voluntary election, or—none at all. I freely confess that the pondering of this question occupied me in the period between bed and sleep, and that I went so far as to make up lists of the electors and the danger from black balls potentially wielded by each. There is certainly a vital anxiety surrounding the entrance to Pop—an anxiety to which the proudest cannot be indifferent, an entrance which the most assured cannot take for granted. To judge by the amount of open courtship which takes place, the volume of self-questioning such as

---

[1] The offer must clearly have been that he should resign his already-won Scholarship to last year's runner-up, who was then disabled from competing by a sudden attack of appendicitis. Patrick would then enter for the examination afresh, and, to appreciate the generosity of the offer, it must be remembered that he would have done so with half of his Divinity work quite unprepared, and the other half 'rusty.'

Patrick Shaw-Stewart.

mine must be proportionately vast. Probably I was one of those accused of courtship. Certainly as the half went on I emerged, to my own astonishment, from tuggish seclusion, and was admitted to the smiles and nods of the main body of Pop, and to the intimacy of its intellectual clique. Further, when these (Charles Lister, Ronald Knox, Robin Laffan, C. A. Gold, Julian Grenfell, with Edward Horner) decided on the venture of an ephemeral paper, they co-opted me in my absence, and together we were committed to the fortunes of the rather notorious *Outsider*. To it I contributed the serial story, various other prose articles, and one or two short efforts in verse. The whole makes, I am ashamed to say, my most considerable literary output to this day. How miserably I have neglected my potentialities! and shall no doubt continue to neglect them if I survive this war. The *Outsider* had peculiar qualities, and its career was contentious from the outset. The social status of the editors, flaringly announced on the comic photographic frontispiece, assured it an initial success, maintained by its conflict with authority. Boomed by much disapproval, it triumphantly carried its bat with six numbers and a credit balance through the Summer half, at the end of which every editor was leaving except myself. From the literary point of view the *Outsider* left much to be desired. It was, of course, crude and youthful, the contributions were sometimes pathetic, and even the work of Charles Lister or Ronald Knox leaned too heavily

Patrick Shaw-Stewart.

on parody. And yet, whenever I read it now I am convulsed with laughter, parental, I suppose.

'For the rest, I played in Middle Club, and occasionally with simple joy (by favour of Julian Grenfell) in Second Upper, inaugurated lawn-tennis in College Field, and enjoyed myself hugely. At the end they all left, Charles Lister, Julian Grenfell, Edward Horner, and the others whom I had made ' my year ' by violence, and was to re-make at Balliol by anticipation. But for the moment I thought I was to fall back on my (rather less diverting) formal contemporaries and juniors for the last and greatest year, the delights of which were pledged to me by my due election to Pop. For the summer holidays (which now seemed almost a flatness between the more significant and delightful halves; so far had the wheel turned) my father had taken a house near Kelso with a few partridges to amuse me. I went back in September (1906), for the beginnings of my last luscious Olympian year.

'The first sensation was one of disappointment at the disappearance of the race of giants, the youth and crudity (albeit attractiveness) of College, and the great density of Oppidan Pop. I had never expected to resent the quality of minnows over whom a reasonable tritonate could be exercised—a weakness I have always strenuously banished—but on this occasion I did so for a time. Soon, however, the joys of pure patronage reasserted themselves, and I revelled in the encouragement of the bashful

Patrick Shaw-Stewart.

and sycophantic minor bloods among whom the rare sparks of intelligence of that period were to be found. I tried unsuccessfully to bully the Keeper into giving me my Mixed Wall outright without regard to St Andrew; I spent my evenings in shining, a revered and slightly fanciful sun, upon the pullulent saplings in Reading-room; I dallied with my candidature for the King's French and German Prizes, and wasted my time as utterly as I had now done for more than a year past. The crisis came on the eve of examination for the King's Prizes: I approached my tutor and blandly suggested scratching for both, on the very reasonable ground that I had not read any of the prepared books. I was prepared for an ado, but not for the sudden, serious turn which it took—the recapitulation of my past idleness, and the suggestion that for my soul's good I should " transfer my sphere of activities " and go straight to Balliol after Christmas, thus gaining a year on life. The prospect of giving up two more halves of glorious ascendancy was almost unbearable (oddly enough the prospect of the Captaincy of the School was neutral now, if not positively unattractive), but by a rather surprising effort which I am inclined to admire in retrospect, I faced it and decided to leave. The remaining month was the most sentimental period of my life. I am not wholly ashamed of the redundancy of my leavetakings. Leaving school is a moment consecrated to these excesses, and I was half-consciously trying to take leave at the

Patrick Shaw-Stewart.
same time of the two still-born halves I had renounced.'

 . . . . . .

The above account gives so complete a picture of Patrick's Eton career that it needs no supplementing from contemporary sources, and if I add a few extracts from his correspondence at the time, it is chiefly in order to give some idea of his literary style and his outlook on life at the period referred to.

 . . . . . .

A Lecture.
'To return to the Tibet lecture, I took Walters to share the delights of the lecture and of my company, which, I hope, he appreciated: we were told all about Tibet, more, far more, than my stammering pen can describe in the two minutes or thereabouts which it has left to stammer in—but the impression left on me was not altogether pleasant, and was that of a rather ferocious, uncivilised, drunken, quarrelsome, dirty, good-for-nothing people who seemed equally opposed to the progress of civilisation and of the missionary—which last fact the gentleman rubbed in with an impressive little pi-gas as a peroration. [FEBRUARY 15, 1902]

'*Chamber*' *as it should be.*
'We have just received notice that the Head, if you please, is going to take prayers to-night, and consequently Chamber is being made into a regular whited sepulchre—stalls irreproachable, Chamber

Patrick Shaw-Stewart.

Table immaculate, with Chamber *Punch* just here, and Chamber *Chronicle* just so, and Chamber *Graphic* just there, the jug and a couple of gallipots just *so* in front of it; the coal messes cleared up, the passage free from all its usual litter, and Chamber, in fact, looking as it never looked before in its life, and never will again! And this—this is what the poor deluded man will consider the usual state of Chamber! [JUNE 18, 1902.]

The Last of the South African War.
' I might tell you how on Monday we were thinking the usual gruesome whole schoolday thoughts, even unto Chapel-time.—But then affairs took a sudden turn.—In Chapel when the usual service was over, we indulged in " Now thank we all our God," and verse one of " God Save the King." I might tell you how, on coming out of Chapel, the Rev. E. Warre, D.D., affixed to the proximity of the notice-board a pamphlet announcing a whole holiday as a result of the news—I might tell you how we returned to Chamber, and there played the big drum on the bottom of our tubs (much to the detriment of the enamel thereon) till Pallis came in and stopped us. I might tell you how I wasted the whole of that glorious day, except a portion of it in which I passed—passed in the watery depths of Cuckoo Weir, where I almost sunk never to rise again in an heroic attempt to tread water, and where, adjured to swim on my back, I almost brought my hard head into harder contact with a hardest punt.

Patrick Shaw-Stewart.

—I might tell you also (this I didn't tell you in my last, for the sequel hadn't happened) how, I repeát, I, and various others in Chamber amused ourselves by propelling water from the windows of Chamber on to the Yards called the School and Weston's respectively; how some of the water thus propelled found its billet into a too close proximity to the head of an old Colleger who was spending Sunday; how the same old Colleger told Pallis; and how, in the evening, we, the perpetrators, were hit by Pallis with a house-cane, seven times hit with grievous violence; and how that makes my fifth.

[JULY 8, 1902.]

At Work.

'I went in for the English Essay Prize last Saturday, without, of course, the slightest chance of getting it, or being mentioned, as all the serious people had been sapping it up since the beginning of the half, and I only began to read up on Wednesday evening, the paper being on Saturday.—The subject was *In Piam memoriam Henrici Sexti regis fundatoris nostri*, and I managed to roll out twenty impassioned pages about that eminently uninteresting monarch's life, period, character, and benefactions, but not, I fear, in a very approved essayist style, as I'd never written one before in my life. Anyway, one gets off an early school, which is a good point!' [NOVEMBER 10, 1903.]

'My tutor informed me the evening we got back that we were all in Upper Division still—which

Patrick Shaw-Stewart.

kindled a ray of hope in my heart! and indeed so we all were in the School List, but in fact we found next day, going to Muggins at 11, that Prior, Morris and I were moved up, and were up to Broadbent at 2.45—so that's the end of that, unless Prior takes a second in Certificate, and I a first (l) he's captain of the school all serene.—My tutor came and apologised to me for being partly responsible, as he had thought it would be worse luck on Prior if we weren't moved up, than for me, if we were, as we had both thought last half would be final.—Broader is a delightful man, rather a wag; he has christened us " The Three Graces," which causes intense merriment to the old established members of the division.'
[APRIL 1, 1904.]

A Postal Order.

'Well, as I think I remarked, that was a most opportune and acceptable P.O.—it was every nice adjective I can think of—it plucked me back from the brink, it set me on my feet again, it started my trousers pockets a-clinking, it made me unashamed to look the world in the face, its " sun scattered the jealous haze " of pecuniary embarrassments, it finally opened and paved with gold the way to the bosom of my family, from three-quarters of which I have so short a time been parted, on Saturday next, June 11th.'   [JUNE 6, 1904.]

Punctuality.

'But I've been, oh! so busy, what with a Field Day on Wednesday and verses hanging on in

Patrick Shaw-Stewart.

consequence till last night—also much of my time is curtailed now by a new system of the Head's, who instead of putting me on Tardy Book for being late for an early school, has made me be in bed by 10.30 for ten days! a singularly irksome expedient.—Another of his measures, which he is just putting into force, is to bar all pumps and slippers out of doors at any time of day or night, which is extraordinarily trying to those who, like me, wear them all day except for Chapel, and rely on them for getting into early school in any time at all.'

[OCTOBER 20, 1905.]

At Play.

'I may mention with pardonable pride that on Friday in College game I played a fine forcing game on a sopping wicket, the bowlers being quite unable to hold the ball, and made twenty-four not out—(*I* think it was at least twenty-eight, but the scorer differed.)' [JUNE 13, 1904.]

'In College Fives, which is drawn for partners on the sheep and goat system, I have drawn quite the best of the goats (one de Bunsen) for partner, and I think we should get through the first round in that. So that all first rounds look rosy, but, alas! " If that were all! "

'With immense energy I beagled last Tuesday, and was in at a most ridiculous death after no run at all—with still greater energy I produced an essay for the Essay Society on Thursday at 9 p.m., on

Patrick Shaw-Stewart.

'"Character in Homer." One is supposed to take some months elaborating these things, and I did all mine but four pages on Wednesday and Thursday! but it went off decently, and was reasonably lengthy—I took over half an hour to read it out to them.'
[FEBRUARY 25, 1905.]

A Halcyon Period.
'Tell my parents from me—especially the maternal—to guard against exaggeration. It is a vice which easily besets us. I am passing an absolutely idyllic existence at present—præpostor at least—and not in for the Divinity part of the Newcastle—so I have no schools, and am not even supposed to be doing any work.' [MARCH 3, 1906.]

Early Militarism.
'I became a bug-shooter last Monday, but only began drill to-day. (8.30—9 a.m., 2.30—3 p.m., and 8—9 p.m.)' [OCTOBER 11, 1903.]

'Soon we marched off down town to the South-Western, where we entrained, the attackers for Sunningdale, and the defenders, us, for Bagshot. There we got out (leaving coats in special, thank goodness!), and marched off smartly for about two and a half miles to the scene of action, with two long spells at the double, which nearly did for me—and others! Arrived there, I crawled about in ditches on my belly, and riddled the enemy with blank fire till, having exhausted my rounds, I was

Patrick Shaw-Stewart.

sent to get more—only to find that all the providers thereof had advanced; so off I skirmished on my own hook till I found my captain (Mr Conybeare), who gave me six more rounds, when all at once the " Cease Fire " sounded and we all trotted off to lunch (a weird collection of cake, bread, cheese, figs, chocolate, cider, etc., rather like an Arab repast!) '
[FEBRUARY 22, 1904.]

' I went and died for my country the day before yesterday—a bad and trying field day. I, with others, was in charge of a convoy, represented by a cart with the big drum in it. Our O.C. took the road he oughtn't to, and was told to wait till he was signalled from on ahead, which we did for half an hour. Then, when he was let go, he rushed us at the double for several sweating miles, at the end of which an angry man on horseback came galloping after us and told us we were going at an impossible pace, and that no convoy could travel at more than three miles an hour, so we must go back and wait again! Afterwards we did a little shooting, but the lunch was the only tolerable incident.'
[OCTOBER 20, 1905.]

Promotion.
' I must make almost unseemly haste to communicate the inspiring news that slow promotion has at last marked me out for its own, and that Edward VII. has need of my services in a higher sphere. All the dignitaries of the E.C.R.V. have dogged my

Patrick Shaw-Stewart.

footsteps for the last week to let me know that there is a commission at my feet if I care to pick it up—and I have replied with suitable dignity that if they really can't do without me, I don't mind if I do. So I shall soon be 2nd Lieutenant P.H.S.S.—most impressive, I call it—only it takes some time, as apparently they have to wait till the departing Lieutenants of last year have sent in their resignations; I shall only be a Sergeant to-morrow for the reception of Haakon—which, incidentally, is, I believe, the last Volunteer function of the half! Still, it is all very delightful.'

[NOVEMBER 11, 1906.]

. . . . . .

There is one accomplishment to which no allusion has been made in any of these extracts which is nevertheless probably one of the chief additions Eton makes to the mental equipment of those who get the best out of her—I mean the power of speaking, or, at least, of lifting up one's voice in public. Although, as will be seen, Patrick did not turn this talent to much account at Oxford, either in the rhetorical or in the histrionic sphere, it is not unlikely that, had he lived, he would have returned to the cultivation of it. He was a valued member of two Shakespeare societies. I think any one who heard him read aloud must agree that, without any very pleasing qualities of voice (his voice was low pitched and rather harsh), he had an extraordinary gift of interpretation. He was also one of the first orators in College Debating Society; and I can still

Patrick Shaw-Stewart.

remember the pathos with which, at the end of a speech defending Greek against Latin, he produced the passage from the *Iliad* in which Helen laments over Hector, the passage which ends :—

σῇ τ' ἀγανοφροσύνῃ καὶ σοῖς 'αγανοῖς ἐπέεσσιν.

But the most characteristic training Etonians get in this direction is that given by 'Speeches' (*i.e.*, recitations) given in Upper School, and, on the Fourth of June, also before a public audience of parents etc. In these performances he took a special pride, and was (I think) especially successful. I think I am right in saying that he once tried the rare experiment of a declamation in Italian.

For, while he had a good schoolboy knowledge of French and German, his preference already lay with Italian, and it was immediately after leaving Eton and before coming up to Balliol that he made his first visit to Italy with the present head master, his tutor at Eton, and Mrs Alington. A few records of this tour are worth preserving :—

'Latterly we have become slightly more proper and classical, with the Palatine (which, unfortunately, poured with rain), the Capitol Museum, and part of the Forum this morning. The Forum excited me more than anything else—and I really did feel a pleasant chill down my spine when I saw the " Lapis Niger," which they have discovered there in the last two years—the inscription on it is undecipherable, but, according to Blakiston, who

Patrick Shaw-Stewart.

knows as much about it as most people, it is in all probability neither more nor less than the tomb of Romulus!

'I am afraid I have rather fallen into the Baedekerian pitfalls, but it is exceedingly hard not to!' [JANUARY 2, 1907.]

'We saw the Holy Cradle (which is really apparently the back of an old Byzantine picture) being exposed in Sta.-Maria Maggiore on Xmas afternoon (the only day in the year it is on view). Those are the sort of things I think one ought to be able to score on heavily in after life when talking to people who think they have seen Rome.'
[JANUARY 2.]

'We had a really Italian dinner last night with one Signor (and Signora) dei Filippi. She was in former life an Americaine, a friend of Mrs Alington's, she has married a Roman chief of balloons (by the way, he wanted us to ascend with him in a balloon, which I was quite keen to do, but Mrs A. said she had to restore me alive to you and wasn't taking any, though I carefully explained that she would be dead too and it wouldn't matter). They gave us a very nice dinner, which had some curious points. Each guest was given a dozen glasses— lovely glasses with gold rim; they poured different wines into every separate glass without the least regard to such minor details as colour. The profusion quite broke my nerve, and I confined

Patrick Shaw-Stewart.
myself to two white varieties. Our teas are most entertaining—we have patronised each best shop in Rome, and the palm is awarded to a German Conditorei which curiously enough resides in the Via Condotti. It is very beautiful, and gives you cream in chocolate *a la* Bunko's.'
[JANUARY 6.]

Of the Italians as a people he seems, like many other travellers, to have derived an unfavourable impression merely on the strength of their trying postal habits. The chief grievance he described in a passage so characteristic at once of his habits and of his style that it must go in in full.

'Philpotts, you know, insisted on sending a spare tooth after me, on the ground that it would not be safe to be in " furrin " parts without a curate. So it duly arrived, and the post office sent me a notice to that effect—(of course, they wouldn't think of such a parergon as *delivering* a parcel). I turned up one morning about half-past ten (immediately after breakfast, in fact), and was met by the astounding intimation that business could only be done " dalle 9 alle 10! " That was too much of a shock, and (as my vicar tooth was still going strong) I let it rip for a week or so. Then came another notice, rather agitated, with " ultimo " written fiercely across it. So, with a tremendous effort, I turned up just before ten, with my tea-cup, so to speak, in one hand, and my bread-and-butter in the other.

Patrick Shaw-Stewart.

After I had waved the beastly ticket in the face of all the wrong officials, one who displayed some slight interest in my fate directed me to a back room, where a stern unwashen man seized my ticket and, after infinite delay, returned with the parcel. Then the troubles began; they demanded a passport, which I didn't possess. Could I prove my identity satisfactorily? I rather feared I could not. Very well, then, they must open the parcel—my heart sank. But, I protested, it is from the dentist britannic; it contains not but one tooth—ah, but one tooth of the most ordinary! It was of no avail. Nothing moved their stony hearts; and with a large penknife the dirtiest and most sinister of the gang proceeded to rip up my parcel. Slowly my wretched tooth was exposed to the light of day; wads of cotton wool were removed, and the wretched article, so to speak, unveiled in the presence of a large and representative gathering. It may have been an impressive spectacle, but it seemed to me in poor taste: and then they weren't satisfied; they began to demand if the tooth did not contain gold—in which case they proposed to charge me at about ten shillings a grain. So I invoked the Virgin and all the saints to witness that the tooth contained nothing but vulcanite and toothiness (which was probably false, as Philpotts is the sort of man who would put gold into tooth-powder on the slightest provocation), and at last escaped with my lovely burden.' [JANUARY 8.]

Patrick Shaw-Stewart.

In connection with these last letters, I cannot help adding a word on a point which the reader of of this chapter might fail to appreciate—and to nobody would that failure in appreciation be more unwelcome than to Patrick himself. In his Eton autobiography, while he does allude, in passing, to the influence of one or two teachers upon his classical progress, he says no word (in the passages which stand in this book) about the more subtle personal influence which masters (and at Eton 'm'tutor' especially) contribute towards the formation of a boy's mind. Such an omission, in any account given by an ordinary person of his schooldays, would probably be due to mere thoughtlessness; the influence of our elders at school is, as a rule, fruitful precisely where and in so far as it is unobtrusive. In Patrick's case I would more willingly attribute it to a strong instinct of reserve, which, while it never led him to spare his own feelings or to excuse his own actions, prevented him from bestowing praise or gratitude which might be unwelcome, because embarrassing, where it was bestowed. Were it not for this, there can be no doubt that the names of his tutor and Mrs Alington would have occurred with more frequency and in more important connections in the foregoing pages. Our contemporaries and those who knew Patrick best will not fail to supply this omission for themselves, but I have felt bound to add this note for the benefit of a larger public.

Chapter Three

I CANNOT attempt to give any description of Patrick's time at Balliol such as he must have given in the lost document which I have referred to in the last chapter —-the continuation of his Eton reminiscences. All I can do is to give some extracts from the letters he wrote to his family at that period illustrating various aspects of his life at that time and his point of view about it. I have not attempted to group or arrange these extracts in any way, preferring to follow merely the order of date; for, indeed, it is one of the most essential features about undergraduate life that its various activities do not (except at certain periods, such as the last few months before Greats) disentangle themselves from one another; we are not bound, as we are bound later in life, to pursue this or that object to the temporary exclusion of others. The strands are inextricably woven together; at half-past four you may be discussing Life and Art with a circle of heavily-minded philosophers; at seven you will be indulging in some more or less orgiastic dinner, the conversation at which is frivolous, or even Fescennine; at a quarter-past nine (for you are probably gated) you attend a meeting of a political society with a gravity that suggests a mind entirely dominated by the subject under discussion. I have left the impressions, then, confused impressions, because that method seems

Patrick Shaw-Stewart.

truest to real life. Only, by way of introduction to the extracts, it is perhaps best to give here some account of the society and of the activities which they refer to.

Patrick never lost sight of the fact that it is academic work which really counts at the University, however little his exterior conduct suggested it. At every moment he had scholastic laurels of one kind or another in his knapsack. When he did his work no one ever quite discovered; he was helped by an amazing facility for reading a book through once and carrying away from it all the profit that other minds would have derived from two or three more hurried and less careful readings; he was also an excellent 'examinee,' and had a quick eye for the main chance in the selection of his reading. This habit of mind he exaggerated himself; he would declare, for instance, that he did not care a straw for the classics, but went on working at them merely because that was the way to get on in life; anybody who knew him knew that this was quite untrue, and there is documentary evidence that he went on reading, and, to some extent, living in the classics (especially his beloved Homer) when all worldly need for the study had long since passed him by. Greek was his preference over Latin, and he only got the Hertford at his second attempt; in the Ireland he won success at the earliest opportunity which could have been expected. His First in Mods. and Greats were a matter of course. But his method of work was not, I should imagine, reassuring

Patrick Shaw-Stewart.

to his tutors: he was always late for lectures, he generally came up on the wrong day, and had to do his Collections (College examinations) at wrong times and in divers places; and there was a flippancy in his style of writing which gave ground for the fear that he would make the fatal mistake of being 'funny' in the examination itself. He never cared much for philosophy; Greek history gripped him, and I think his most generous efforts were devoted to it. He and I read all through Aristophanes together, writing out and committing to memory all the numerous allusions in his works to contemporary politics, and Patrick actually took this as a 'special subject' in the Schools.

His political views were pronounced, but he had not enough power of throwing himself into make-believe to figure very prominently in the rather dingy microcosm of undergraduate politics. His voice was not well suited for addressing a large audience, and his jokes were often too esoteric for a Union public. But he was a welcome speaker among the mulled-claret-cups of the Canning, and he insisted on being elected to the 'Orthodox,' a Socialist creation of Charles Lister's, in spite of a total absence of political sympathy; his energies here were chiefly directed to black-balling earnest candidates (of unimpeachable sentiments), on the ground that they were not jolly. He occasionally held office in College debating societies, but generally to their detriment, for the future financier was marked out by a glorious lack of anything like

Patrick Shaw-Stewart.

organising capacity: in one case, summoned to a special meeting to face a vote of censure on the ground of a term's neglect, he arrived by mistake a quarter of an hour too early, and found no members present, only two large jugs of claret cup; these (thinking it a pity they should be wasted) he carried off to Stair XIV., and consumed with his intimates, while a thirsty society passed its vote *nem. con.* Politics added spice to life, but he never contemplated taking them seriously till he should have gained a solid position in the world.

Rowing appealed to two sides of his nature as being at once patriotic and fashionable, and despite all resistances of nature he submitted to its inconveniences without the hope of ever achieving fame in this direction. He dabbled in most other forms of athletics (Oxford makes no provision for racquets, his real game: I doubt if he played real tennis much till after he had taken his degree).

But, above all, his nature was sociable, and he would pay less attention to the things he did than to the people he did them with. To make new acquaintances, to find himself in new *milieux*, to appear, to shine, to captivate, these were his arts. Not that he flung his nets wide at Oxford; the only social event which exercised him particularly was his election to the Annandale ('Anner'), a Balliol dining-club. But already, in the Vacations, he was beginning that round of country-house parties and London balls which was to become a habit with him. The reading-party at Brancaster in the summer of

Patrick Shaw-Stewart.

1907 was really his debut; from that time onwards the centre of his life lay quite as much away from Oxford as in it, and the end of the term no longer brought him, as the end of the half at Eton used to bring him, its regrets.

But while it is possible thus to reconstruct in some degree the background of his habits, it would need far more powers of description to attempt any such portrait of the friends in whose circle he moved at Balliol. Those who have read the memoirs of Charles Lister and of the Grenfell brothers, will have caught something of the atmosphere, but it is only preserved in fragments. To read these extracts from Patrick's letters with full understanding, you should have some picture of Charles Lister, with his generous enthusiasms, his reckless fun, his nervous breeziness of manner, his embarrassing conviction that every second person he met was a 'good chap,' his bewildering organisations, his despairing jeremiads, his inexhaustible vitality. Of Julian Grenfell with his game-book, his stock-whip, his greyhounds, his highly intellectualised contempt of intellect, replaced afterwards by an unformed but passionate philosophy, his intolerance of people he did not know, his wild high spirits, and compensating depressions. Of Edward Horner, most generous of hosts and most enthusiastic of companions, a prophet of ecstasy; to Patrick himself a fellow-Meredithian; in politics, despite all protests from his friends, an unabashed Whig. Of Victor Barrington-Kennett ('B.-K.'), huge and formidable, until you realised

Patrick Shaw-Stewart.
that his formidability was shyness; whimsical in humour, open-hearted and direct of speech, fascinating even where he did not attract. Of George Fletcher (' Hoj '), not altogether of the same circle, yet always an intimate of Patrick's, with his pose of rustic uncouthness, his blunt manner, his little disapproving snort, his extravagant loyalty for the institutions which fostered him, captain of the school at Eton in Patrick's last term, and afterwards, there and at Shrewsbury, best beloved of schoolmasters. All these came to Balliol the term before Patrick, all have given up their lives in the same cause with him. There are others, too, needed to complete the picture; some of them seniors, jealously at first but afterwards generously welcoming into their circle this sudden and violent infusion of new Eton blood—such was Douglas Radcliffe, who was elected with Patrick to All Souls', and died at Hooge; some of them are juniors, Billy Grenfell and John Manners and their friends, eager to catch up and perhaps to develop unnecessarily the tradition that was only the tradition of a clique. Had Patrick's account of his Balliol days survived, he would have left us a more personal record of these friends than the reader will derive for himself from casual allusions in letters written to people who were supposed to know the names already.

Patrick's father died on July 6, 1908; his mother on Dec. 22, 1909. In September the family moved to Carnock, in Stirlingshire.

Patrick Shaw-Stewart.

First Impressions.
'. . . Since then I have floated into the usual Oxford existence—easy-going, digestive, conversational, unathletic, and very amusing. I seem to have talked for years to every Old Etonian in this college, and they are by no means few—I have arranged to have lunch regularly with Ronald, Hoj, and Horner.'
[JANUARY 23, 1907.]

Examination for the Hertford Scholarship.
'Thursday, Friday, and Saturday were stern and grim. Papers 9.30 to 12.30 and 2 to 5; and if there is one thing I bar more than another, it is a paper at 2 after a heavy luncheon (of course I always have to feed up during an exam.). The papers were terrible; I never met anything in my life that showed up my ignorance of Latin at large so lamentably as the General Paper. I think I have had about enough Latin now to keep me going for a year—why can't they have a Greek exam.? In the course of the last paper, on Saturday afternoon, there was one of the most tremendous thunderstorms I ever came across—hailstones and coals of fire. It was most annoying, as I could neither attend properly to the thunderstorm nor write decently at my paper, especially in pitchy darkness. It really is about time we had a little summer now, but the thunderstorm hasn't produced the slightest effect yet.' [JUNE 3, 1907.]

Patrick Shaw-Stewart.
Recreations.

'Oxford would be an excellent place in the summer if summer showed the slightest disposition to come on—as it does nothing but blow and rain, there are drawbacks. All the same, I have got in two games of tennis, and several nautical expeditions on the Char, in which I am putting in a rather tortuous apprenticeship in the art of punting.

'Charles and Ronald and Jack Horner and Wilfred Knox and I share a punt at the cost of £1 each for the term, which is not exorbitant, considering the usage it undergoes at our hands—we being all embryo punters and inclined to butt the banks. Charles punting is a sight for the gods—the other day he left his pole sitting upright in the water, and only by the grace of Heaven failed to leave himself sitting on the top of it.

'Julian, who is a sort of amateur punting champion, took us out one day to show us how it ought to be done, but his example has not yet had any striking effects. To-day I am actually going to play cricket—for the Balliol Erratics v. Abingdon. The calibre of the Erratics may be estimated from the fact that the order of going in is decided by lot—but this is usually concealed from the opposition.'

[SUMMER TERM, 1907.]

The Hertford Result.

'Ronald has gone and got the Hertford. I am glad it was Ronald, and not some horrible man.

Patrick Shaw-Stewart.

' Last Thursday to Saturday was a great bore, two three-hours papers every day—and I was glad when it was over. I thought I had done fairly well, but was sure there were lots of curious men who could beat us both.' [JUNE 5, 1907.]

The Fourth of June at Eton, and other matters.
' Finally Charles gave his people and the Mannerses and me a supper in the garden of an extraordinary little Eton pot-house called The Sun, which I had never previously explored; so like Charles, it was very amusing, the sort of meal where caterpillars fall off overhanging trees into the mint sauce, and mangy cats prowl round for morsels. Charles and I didn't stay for fireworks—others did, and subsequently clomb into College—but I thought that performance, besides being agonisingly athletic, would not go well with my best new clothes: I tried it once, and never was so uncomfy in my life.

' The dinner in the Hall to the new master was quite impressive; all his old pupils were there (of whom the Vice-Chancellor is one!), and he made an exceedingly long and quite adequate oration.

' On Sunday the master was installed in Chapel and Gore preached a jolly sermon: Ronald had him to lunch, where he was as usual delightful and marvellously unclerical. Father Waggett came in afterwards, just missed him, but stayed a good hour: so I enjoyed the company of two rather distinguished ecclesiastics—Ronald, by the way, is to give us a dinner in honour of his Hertford, which I tell him

Patrick Shaw-Stewart.
will just nicely account for one year's value of it.

'Talking of dinners, I have been invited to join the " Caledonian Club," which I am sure will ruin me, as its only *raison d'être* appears to be large dinners about once a term: but I can't resist it, as you have to wear a perfectly fascinating green dinner-jacket with purple facings representing the thistle.

'I was at Eton again yesterday, playing cricket against College; a most exciting match. They made 150 for 6 and declared, leaving us an hour, and we beat them on the stroke of time. Alington made a wonderful innings of 90 not out for us (we won by one wicket, by the way). I made ten, and was much pleased with myself. I enclose the Hertford papers—also the Caledonian rules—which please return.'   [JUNE 12, 1907.]

The Noiseless Tenour.
'Life here has been pretty noiseless-tenorous; the Caledonian dinner, I discovered, had come off previously, so I shall have to wait till St Andrew's Day for the first official display of my beautiful new garment, but I shall wear it unofficially for your delectation in the Vac. The " Annandale " dinner came off last Wednesday, and was moderately jolly; there was some feeling afterwards because an ecstatic Balliol man after dinner threw three bowls from Balliol Quad. through a window in Trinity. The Trinity man took and showed them to a don of sorts, and explained that they had destroyed two

Patrick Shaw-Stewart.

or three valuable works of art, and very nearly his own valuable life. That Trinity man is not popular in Balliol nowadays. Slight unwonted intellectual activity at present because of "Collections" to-morrow and next day.' [JUNE 20, 1907.]

End-of-Term Comments.

'My end-of-term exam. papers went off quite well on the whole, as I got "alpha minus" for each of them, and had quite a satisfactory "hand shaking" —I think I described the third-person process to you. Well, this time Cyril said to the Master, "Mr S.-S. has been very satisfactory—he was distinguished in the Hertford exam., did good collection papers, has done some nice comps. for me, and some particularly good papers on Homer—however, I should like to recommend him to be a little more regular in his work, and consult the times of others more than his own" (this, I suppose, meant shirking Lectures), "as it is, I suppose he has some mysterious time of day when he works, but I have never been able to discover it: I fear he has other interests than his work."

'So the Master said, "Oh, is his time taken up by societies?"

'"Well," said Cyril, "I think he is a figure not unknown in societies and society."

'The Master didn't catch on to that, and said, "Well, Mr S.-S., of course these societies are excellent in their way, but you must remember you have all your life to devote to philanthropy, or

Patrick Shaw-Stewart.
whatever you are keen on" (I smiled at that, I suppose he thinks I am a Socialist) " whereas your four years at Oxford are your only chance of making yourself an educated man."

'So I said I would be sure to make myself one, and bowed out.' [JUNE 22, 1907.]

The Brancaster Reading-party.

'The next day was the opening of the great reading-party—went down to Brancaster after lunch, and was motored to the Farm. Now, that reading-party was all very well as a picnic—but d——d poor for reading. To begin with, we knew each other too well, consequently talked, not read (mean to go on next reading-party with bores).

'Then there were the Ribblesdales literally within a stone-throw. Then the Magdalen reading-party, with Alan Parsons in it, round the corner, and then the Trees 100 yards down the road. All elements of disturbance, golf, bathing, dinners—anything but work. Then again we were within reach of London, which was fatal. The Friday of that week was the great Taplow water-party—so what could I do? Needless to say I went, had a lovely time, two and a half hours in a pair canoe.'

[AUGUST, 1907.]

'The last week at Brancaster was much like its fellows—quiet, studious reading, with a slight fillip of female society. We bathed nearly every day—frightfully rough sometimes but extremely

Patrick Shaw-Stewart.

salubrious. I feel quite offensively healthy as a general result of the place. I bathed in pyjamas at first till I could raise a bathing dress, pyjamas are elegant enough in their way, but have rather a drowned rat appearance after the bath. The Ribblesdales had Alfred Lyttleton the first week-end, whom I liked awfully.' [AUGUST 7, 1907.]

A Paper for the Canning.
'I had a strenuous time the early part of last week. The Canning on Sat. suddenly found it wanted a paper read to it on Wed. Wolmer went round to every one, including me. I thought it was an excellent opportunity for acquiring merit, as I knew that however long I was given, I shouldn't begin it till the day beforehand, so I undertook it, began on Tues. evening, but wrote practically all of it on Wed., up till the last moment, in fact. I chose "The next Hague Conference," as not requiring much preparation and as giving a chance for fine old Jingo invective on the achievements of the last, and on Peace in general—but most of the paper was in the lighter vein and had an undeserved vogue, as some of the audience got hysterical in the first minute or two, and were ready to laugh at anything.' [AUTUMN, 1907.]

This paper has been preserved. It was fascinating as a performance, but it shows traces in its style of the high speed at which it was written, and the humour is largely esoteric. But it seems well to

Patrick Shaw-Stewart.
subjoin here part of the peroration because, however hastily written, it certainly represents Patrick's considered views on war as a factor in civilisation.

'The necessity and the desirability of war are both in nature: arbitration and peace have their origin in the art of enervated mankind; peace that is in so far as it is not spontaneous, not the involuntary holding up of the hands in token of surrender, or the mutual pause of utter weariness. The fallacy which needs to be controverted is that war is a relic of barbarism, a savage, primitive, and uncivilised condition out of which mankind is destined to grow. Nothing could be further from the reality. War is as much an elementary and permanent instinct of human nature as is love; and its complete cessation would be followed with an almost equal rapidity, if less directly by the extinction of the race. It is as idle to condemn war because of the undoubted misery and suffering which it causes, as it would be to condemn the reproduction of our kind on account of the pains of childbirth.

'The benefits of war to the combatants themselves are so obvious as hardly to need recapitulation. Were a late distinguished member of this Club present to-day, it would ill beseem a mere civilian to dilate upon the South African War: but mercifully, owing to the widespread popularity of the works of Mr Kipling, the thrills of patriotism may be acquired by the mildest of men with little trouble and practically no expense. In a single word, to

Patrick Shaw-Stewart.

the trained soldier war is his *raison d'être*, his *apologia pro vita sua*: to the volunteer it is the opportunity for the most splendid self-sacrifice that it commonly falls to the lot of mankind to make. To the nation at large it is practically the only influence which can shake the average citizen out of his self-absorbed tranquillity. He is carried away by the tide: his pulses are quickened despite himself: he must "be constant in our ills, and joyous in our joy." Any of us who cannot even now feel the black misery of that week when Stormberg, Colenso, and Magersfontein followed one another in ghastly procession, or the frenzy of resistance when the fate of Ladysmith trembled in the balance, can only be pitied. Nor is it in the least pertinent to sneer at the mournful fact that popular demonstrations of joy consequent upon British successes confined themselves mainly to smacking old men on the back with inflated bladders and tickling girls in the street with peacock-feathers. "For things like that, you know, must be after a famous victory." The crudity of the demonstrations represented merely the spasmodic movements of the nation rousing itself from phlegmatic slumber, the grunts of the awakening voice, trying to articulate its delight. We shall do better another time, like the Hague Conference, but unlike them, it was too much time for preparation that hampered us—and after all, a war of aggression across two continents is not calculated to arouse the noblest national enthusiasm. Finally, the beauty of war, if so it

Patrick Shaw-Stewart.

may be phrased, is that a state of actual war is far from necessary for a realisation of its benefits. It is the contingent possibility of a state of war that renders the intervals of peace no less salutary to the nation than the most ensanguined battlefield. It is the possibility of war, though it may be as remote as we are assured that it is to-day, that fosters the national spirit, the spirit of independence, the spirit of competition which is the animant spirit of the human race, the *mens agitans molem et magno se corpore miscens.*'

An Interlude.
'On Thursday evening, being Nov. 5th, there were " rags " everywhere. Fireworks are sat upon at Balliol as dangerous to the buildings, so we bought a little black pig, and introduced him into College: he ran like a hare into Senior Common Room among the assembled dons! but he was certainly great fun. We had a most hilarious evening, and made an enormous temple of crockery in the quad. where we worshipped with due ceremony—that pleased the dons a great deal; they are really very good chaps in that way. They (represented by the Junior Dean) merely made a little oration to us afterwards about examples, etc., in the course of which he said we were all " prominent men," which pleased Edward tremendously—he said he had never been called that before in his life.

'There was great difficulty, by the way, as to where the pig should spend the night, ultimately

Patrick Shaw-Stewart.
Julian wrapped him up in his best dressing gown! We had to buy him outright (for £2), as the man said if you took him out of the litter, and then put him back, the others would rag him! Anyhow, he's fattening him for us now, and we shall have a "pig-supper" soon. [NOVEMBER, 1907.]

Patrick's Ireland.
'The Ireland is getting very near and very horrible, but I know I shall enjoy the exam. itself— I always do!

'It begins to-day week, so you will know when to begin concentrating your will-power.'
[DECEMBER, 1907.]

The Old Etonian Dinner.
'I don't think Balliol were very popular at the function—they sat together very distinctively in a corner which they had secured beforehand, and were as usual arrogant, noisy, and uncompromising— also they were all wearing old clothes as a protest against the fashionable departures of Magdalen and New College. After dinner we danced very elegantly to the strains of the Town Band, I was considerably in request in a female rôle. I am rowing at present, and I am standing up to write! However, I think I shall soon be turned out after the 2nd Torpid, and then my sorrows will end.'
[FEBRUARY 4, 1908.]

Patrick Shaw-Stewart.
A Variety of Engagements.
'Last Saturday there was a big O.E. dinner here, to which about 70 people went, organised, of course, by Marsden.

'Balliol increased, no doubt, their Varsity popularity by sitting all together in a corner, aloof, noisy, and arrogant.

'I've had an instructive week of it.

'Tues. evening a discussion on Nietzche at the Orthodox; Wed. evening a paper by Cyril (lantern slides), on Botticelli; Thursday the Union, on the Liberal Government, at which I spoke. I spoke at considerable length and with moderate éclat. The Union, of course, took all the wrong points, and missed all the good ones, as it always does.

'I gave a little political dinner to Ronald (who's now Secretary) and Wolmer before it.

'I've got my rowing *congé* now, and do nothing but occasional tennis and golf—and work, of course.' [FEBRUARY, 1908.]

An Echo of the Past.
'Then on Friday I came here for my Rest before "Mods.," and to see Basil before he went back. That evening he and W. and I went to a Free Trade meeting at Queen's Hall, addressed by Lloyd George. W. had to have a special "Ladies' Pass" to prove she wasn't a Suffragette, and even so, five burly policemen closed in ominously round her as she approached. We were so late that our seats

Patrick Shaw-Stewart.

were taken, and we were right at the back, immediately behind the three most zealous and least presentable supporters of Free Trade I ever came across. L. George spoke quite fairly well—good manner, bad matter, and a totally irrelevant peroration about pruning hooks and the Prince of Peace —and 2 Suffragettes and 7 Protectionists were ejected in the course of the speech.' [MARCH, 1908.]

Patrick's First in Mods.
'All is over. I have fought the g.f. and showed up my last Mods. paper at 5 p.m. on Thursday, and glad I was to do it. I think I've got a fairly Heygate 1st—at least it'll be a very good joke if it's a Brahms 2nd,* but I don't think it will be— and as for a Brahms " good " 1st, I neither want it nor expect it—my theory being that one could only want it either for show (which wouldn't apply as nobody knows what sort of 1st you get) or for private satisfaction: which personally I should never get out of a prepared books exam. So " Ta." '
[MARCH, 1908.]

Charles Lister in Florence.
' I think Cyril Bailey was rather relieved when C. departed—while he was there one never quite knew what was going to happen next. One evening he made us go to a curious performance of *Carmen*,

---
* 'Brahms' is an echo of a Balliol vocabulary which replaced descriptive epithets by the names of musicians. 'Brahms' meant 'recherché,' 'out of the common'—the opposite of 'Handel.'

Patrick Shaw-Stewart.

finishing up at a low German beer hall, where C. drank vats of Munich beer and discussed Theology and politics. Another evening to a cinematograph performance of the *Life of Jesus* (which, I'm bound to say, was extremely good), and on a third evening he sat down so heavily on his bed that it collapsed beneath the impact. Little things like this contributed to do for Cyril's reputation in the hotel, which had previously been unimpeachable.'

[APRIL, 1908.]

Assisi.

' All this, as I say, till yesterday when we suddenly moved here, as if on purpose to exhaust one's stock of superlatives. The bad weather had more or less given way in Florence, but yesterday was exceptionally good, and we walked up from the station at 10 p.m., suddenly plunged into mountain air after the hot, stuffy Val d'Arno and the hot, stuffy train, with a full moon, and a mackerel sky, and Assisi perched on the hill in front of us, looking different to anything else. I should think Schoolyard, and the Parthenon (the former of which I *have* seen by moonlight, the latter not!) are the only things in the same class.' [APRIL, 1908.]

The Return from Florence.

' Two hours ago I left Florence crying large and numerous tears the while. Never have I got to love a place so in ten days. Florence is so small, and unspoiled, and *gemuthlich* or *avenant*, or

Patrick Shaw-Stewart.

whatever one calls it, that I've quite lost my heart to it, and fully intend to return there at the earliest possible opportunity—that is, when I feel rich enough. For, at present, I'm absolutely broke—hence my precipitate return, the fact being that I'm fleeing the devil in the shape of Porto Fino, which would mean Heaven knows how much more disbursement. As it is, I shall probably complete my bankruptcy by staying a night in Milan—but I simply must do that, there are so many things to see there, including the lady who hangs on my wall at Balliol.' [APRIL 18, 1908.]

The Return to Oxford.
 'I'm afraid this is rather late, but the effort of conforming to the comparatively regular ideas of life obtaining in this Ancient University has been so severe that little trifles like correspondence have gone by the board.
 Beginning with Taplow, there were the Manners twins and Venetia Stanley and Archie Gordon, also Lord Hugh Cecil and Winston. I distinguished myself by nearly drowning one of the twins in the weir, and being late for dinner when I was to take my hostess in. On Monday I came straight on here. The College seemed quite pleased to see me, even at a time of my own choosing; they have plunged me swiftly in the vortex of greats. I now go to a lecture on " Moral Philosophy " with Rashdall, who talks about " the form of the moral law," and the " concept of conscience," and to one

Patrick Shaw-Stewart.

on the Republic also at New College, where I am told about " customary virtue being inadequate," and that, as a rule, " ortogeny follows phylogeny." All very edifying. Also our own Master on " Roman Constitutional History," frightful hair-splitting, about the exact status of the client and the manumitted slave in Early Republican Times. However, I suppose this is how one's mind gets broadened.' [MAY, 1908.]

His New Home at Carnock.—To his Nurse.
' This is a perfectly lovely place. You will love it when you see it. A perfectly proportioned old house in that delicate dirty-gray colour, with no visible front door, and the two funny breakneck winding stone staircases. You must come soon and see it. Wouldn't Father have loved it ? You know he says a lot about it in one of those old letters.'
[SEPTEMBER 29, 1908.]

His Politics.
' I haven't time to enlarge on that just now, as the post is going every minute, except just to say that my politics are as pliable as you could possibly desire them—only you'll admit it's rather difficult to make a mark as a youthful statesman, and at the same time to abstain from belonging to any party! besides the fact that I'm already Secretary of the foremost Tory Club in Oxford—however——'
[OCTOBER, 9, 1908.]

Patrick Shaw-Stewart.

Various Engagements.

'This must be brief, because I am really busy just at present, and particularly hard driven to-day, as I have been away at Eton playing the Wall Game against College for Laffan's scratch—(we were defeated, I'm sorry to say)—and now must go in 10 min. to the Canning to hear a paper on DRINK, and then I have to write a belated essay on the Political Loyalty of Sulla, and then begin to compose the speech I've rashly undertaken to make to-morrow at the Union, "That Asquith's Unemployed Proposals are utterly inadequate." As I have to open the debate, I can't rely on what my opponents say, and must make up the whole speech beforehand. So you will allow that my time is mapped out, if not cut out, for the moment.'

[OCTOBER 28, 1908.]

Rebuffs.

'That, however, is only a part of the buffetings of Fate, as I have been degraded to a tiny part in the Greek play for next term, and am in immediate danger of being turned out of the 2nd Balliol "Togger" boat. Hence I have decided that the world is a hollow sham, and turned inwards on myself—however, I dare say I shall turn out again when the Canning paper is finished.

'Meanwhile, I row and row, and read the lessons in Chapel, and attend "smoking concerts" at various colleges, which come in a heap now—Trinity last night, Univ. this.' [? AUTUMN, 1908.]

Patrick Shaw-Stewart.
A Caledonian Dinner.
'Life has been profoundly uneventful since I came back from London—eating, sleeping, rowing, and a little working—the eating occasionally more or less solemnised, as at the Caledonian dinner on Wednesday, when we all turned up in our thistle-coloured jackets, and ate haggis and Athol brose, and had our food piped down our throats, and afterwards, when we were sufficiently ecstatic, danced reels and schottisches.'
[NOVEMBER, 1908.]

Eating Bar Dinners.
'I am wallowing in a deluge of legal documents, some to be signed by me to say I'm not in Holy Orders, nor a Solicitor, nor in any capacity similar or analagous to that of a Solicitor—and so on for a page and a half of close print, ending with "nor am I engaged in trade, nor am I an undischarged bankrupt," which has a gleam of fun in it; others to be signed by the Master, and others again by old and crusted barristers to say they like my looks—these I have sent to Evan and Raymond. The upshot is that I go to dear Connie on Friday till Monday. Probably they won't allow me to eat dinners when I get there, as not having been up for 2 years, but anyway I shall get the leave, and as Green Street, Arlington Street, Bedford Square, and Chiswick are all, I believe, humming with life, what I say is, why not?'
[NOVEMBER, 1908.]

Patrick Shaw-Stewart.

The Grindstone.

'When I came up in my leisurely way on the Monday I was given 2 enormous Colleccers to do, which I have had to put in at odd times ever since—(really one term I shall try doing them at the normal time as a labour-saving!)—and what between wrestling with their inquiries on the distinction between Real and Unreal pleasures, and doing an Essay for J. A. Smith on Aristotle's Conceptions of Happiness viewed in the light of Mills' "Utilitarianism," I really have lived among dogmas for the last few days!'

[JANUARY 25, 1909.]

In Training.—To his Mother.

'About 7.25 I arise and fling myself into shorts and sweater and GO FOR A RUN—back at 8, bracing cold bath—breakfast at 8.20 (food carefully selected). Then work—there being nothing else to do at that appalling hour—from 9 to 11. Lunch at 1 (again all muscle-building in accordance with the latest principles), then down to the river at 2.30 and tug my oar till 4, then run round Christ Church meadows, then tea—then work till 7—then a dinner consisting mainly of toast and lettuce and Brussels sprouts—then more work—then——

'BED AT 10.30.

'Do you recognise your son? and yet I assure you it's the solemn Truth.'

[SPRING, 1909.]

Patrick Shaw-Stewart.
A Fourth of June at Eton.
'I've been leading the dedicated life quite consistently this week—last Friday a slight gaiety, if the wettest fourth of June on record can be so described. Considering the uninterrupted downpour I don't think I managed my day so very ill. It contained speeches (without a ticket), luncheon with Ainger, a game of racquets in the afternoon, tea with John Manners, and dinner at Tap with Lady Salisbury. Last 4th of June I got the Hertford, and the one before I was elected to the Anner: so that I've got to associate it in my mind with violent head-turning. Add to this the indefatigable rain, you will at once, with your usual acumen, perceive that it fell slightly short of the high record of that glorious anniversary.'

[JUNE 11, 1909.]

A Reading Party at Petertavy.
'I ended London jollily with an ultra-smart cotillon at Mrs Cavendish Bentinck's, and the King and Queen ball at Doncaster House. After that anything further would have been a bathos, and a graceful retirement to rustic seclusion became imperative. On Monday I beat a graceful retreat by the 3.30 and found myself here at a sort of supper after an interminable drive. Edward and Twiggy Anderson are here already, and Jasper Ridley arrives to-day. I think we're all marvels of renunciation, don't you? and if you could see our régime!! my day begins with a dip *in the river*

Patrick Shaw-Stewart.

at 7.45, and ends briskly at 10.30. It's so funny (and no doubt so salutary) after 3 weeks of bed at 3.30, and up at 12.' [JULY, 1909.]

In Digs at 8 Long Wall.
  'This will have to be rather in haste, but it's all important it should reach on Saturday—at least that's the tradition I cling to from earliest Eton.
  'I think my last letter contained Gisburne and touched on Oxford, so there is only my quiet, steady daily life remaining, which, as you know, is pestered with philosophy, but slightly helped by history. We've settled into 8 Long Wall pretty well now, and I really like it quite a lot. The cuisine is very fair, and our little shared valet quite an excellent man.' [OCTOBER 22, 1909.]

  'My rooms really look extremely jolly—the rooms of a scholar and a gentleman; "Lewis" Waller looks blooming and lends an air of rather *recherché* 18th Centuryism, and Balzac is perfectly supreme, it hits every one in the eye as they come in. BUT there are one or two alarming gaps in my mental catalogue. The Ancient Mariner, for instance, is nowhere to be found, and I'm terribly afraid that, lying as he did all over the bottom of a Tate's cube sugar, he may have done protective mimicry and got lost, which would simply break my heart. Then there is Petrarca, Vol. I, bound in green cloth. I had him with me on my travels, and expect he is at Carnock—if not, I fear he is in

Patrick Shaw-Stewart.

one of the Homes of England, which Heaven forfend. Then there is the question of Dante—I seem to remember intending to have Grandfather's, and then one of Father's turning up, but I can't remember which I decided to bag, and worse still, NEITHER is here; can you throw any light on that?' [NOVEMBER, 1909.]

Prospects of Greats Work.

'For instance, I got an " Alpha " (tho' a very much qualified one) in the logic paper in collections this time—and as that is easily far and away my weakest point, it's quite pleasant.

'The Greek history paper, on the other hand, wasn't quite as successful as I had thought, but that was because the examiner disagreed with me on every point, and Lindsey, at hand-shaking, said to the Master, " Of course, Mr S.-S. thinks nothing of philosophy " (I wonder how they've all got that into their head), " but I think he will be very good at it all the same."

'So much for that—it doesn't prevent this vac. being a gloomy prospect of 8 hours a day, which I shall put in part at Carnock, part (more grimly) at Mells, with Edward and Ronald—excellent companions, but for a dismal task!

'I have refused everything—it is sickening to have to do it, isn't it, you *do* agree with me, I know —it's really enormous heroism, but wholly unrequited, and people merely think it silly—that's the fatal part of having the reputation of a " clever."

Patrick Shaw-Stewart.
'People say, "Oh, absurd! *you* could do it all in six weeks," and when you try to explain that six weeks is on the short side for imbibing theories about Time and Eternity, they don't believe you, and think it's *them* in particular you're shirking. Such is life.

'If it's successful, I suppose it justifies itself, but I swear if I get a 2nd after this, I shall take off my boots and go to bed.' [DECEMBER, 1909.]

Gisburne.
'What do you think I've been doing to-day? No—one. No—two. I've been out with the Ribblesdale Buck hounds, and oh, my dear, the agony of those parts that bear most of the contact between man and horse is indescribable.

'But I feel a tremendous "sporman," and triumphant despite my exhaustion. Yesterday I would have shot pheasants in the morning had I not unfortunately overslept, and in the afternoon we coursed with Diana's long dogs!

'So life is strenuous.' [DECEMBER 18, 1909.]

Mells.
'Edward had arrived on Monday, and Ronald yesterday evening. We've done quite a lot of work, and Edward has called on his aunts: Sir John's cellar is a great acquisition to any Reading Party. It was sad to go away from you two——in some

Patrick Shaw-Stewart.

ways it's as well I'm always in such a desperate hurry at the anguished moment of departure.'

[JANUARY, 1910.]

The 1910 *Election.—To his Nurse.*
' I am, as you know, one of those vulgar people who aren't much good at the subtler issues of politics, but are simply thrilled to the bone by a General Election.

' I was awfully disappointed the first few days when there weren't nearly enough gains, but yesterday the shires were perfectly splendid, and I'm just off now to the Union to see if any of this morning's counts are out yet.

' Dear, why is Scotland so terribly Radical, it is very saddening to me, but I was glad to see Kirkcudbright was won yesterday, and 2 seats in Wales, so the " Celtic Fringe " is decreasing a little—but there are some bad Scottish industrial centres to come yet. Now I must run and play golf.

' Oh, Dear! Wick Burghs are as bad as Ross and Cromarty, and they included Dingwall, Cromarty Town, and Tain, didn't they? I think it's just disgraceful, after they returned a Unionist in 19 6, even. Well, well, I don't think Edward R₀ is going to create 400 Liberal Peers anyway, and I shall fight for him if he refuses.

' So there.' [FEBRUARY, 1910.]

Patrick Shaw-Stewart.

An Attack of Mumps.
'This morning my other cheek showed signs of impending symmetry. Waterhouse plumped for that odious disease whose very name is a laughing stock and which I would sooner die than write down—having already " blushed it through " the telegraph office. So the issue is now clear, and I must face a week or so of this very humiliating position. Edward, etc., sallied out and hired me a nurse this morning, not that I afford her very much employment, but it's just as well the servants shouldn't be in or out. She is an admirable woman of superhuman energy though but small physical attractions. She has just performed entirely single-handed the gigantic labour of taking my bed to pieces and carrying it upstairs and putting it in here (here being my sitting-room upstairs).'
[JANUARY 24, 1910.]

An Illness of his Sister.
' This is a sad thing to think of you in bed—and much more in bed than me, who get up at 12.30 daily and stay up till ever so late. I tell you plainly I don't like it: you're trying to cut me out as an invalid—I did think I was established as *the* invalid of the family for months to come. It's an awful-like thing really, and for the Lord's sake, tinged with mine, don't travel too soon, or you really *will* cut me out as an invalid—probably anticipate me in that undeveloped land of St Ninian's, so don't.'
[JANUARY 28, 1910.]

Patrick Shaw-Stewart.
Prospects for the ' Jenks.'—To his Nurse.

'I am sorry to have given you such a sudden shock and then never explained about it, but really I haven't had a *moment*: haven't now, for the matter of that. I have been pushed very hard to finish my verses for the (Greek) Gaisford Prize, which I have sent in to-day. They aren't very good, which is a bore: but in any case it doesn't come out for 2 months!! so one needn't worry about it much. No sooner is that finished than I have to go in for the Jenkyns Exhibition ("the Jenks"), which begins at the end of this week. This year I am only playing with it, as I know no philosophy, so it won't be so very alarming—still I must try and read up a few things before it begins. I shan't have a peaceful moment from now till June year, and even then it'll only be the beginning of something else. Oh, Dear, how I do hate work!'

[MARCH 1, 1910.]

Facts about the ' Jenks.'

' 1. That the standard was the highest of recent years.

' 2. That all the 5 people on the list were close together and very hard to place.

' 3. That Ronald got it on his philosophy, and not his classics, which were not as good as mine.

' 4. That my philosophy was quite good, probably the best after his.

' 5. That my history was not so good, and my essay on Art and Truth was too funny, and that

Patrick Shaw-Stewart.

pulled me down—(I knew it was, but I don't repent, for I could not have really gripped the subject).

'6. That I am " quite safe " for Greats.'
[MARCH 17, 1910.]

King Edward's Funeral.
' I arrived before 9, but I really believe I might have been much later. There I found a great black company on the Terrace, including all the Grenfells, except Julian—I always think women look best in black. Well, we waited, and waited, and nothing seemed to happen, except Colonial contingents. It was strangely unlike the bitter cold at Victoria's funeral—to-day a cloudless sky, great heat, and mercifully trees above our heads, which shaded us without blocking the view. Suddenly we realised that the gunners were trailing past, the bands beginning to be audible, and after that I was transfixed, it wasn't a bit pathetic (all the pathos they say was at Tuesday's removal) but infinitely splendid. The most curious difference from 1901 was that, as the sun was bright, the Crown and the Orb *shone*, and the whole thing looked glittering instead of dark. [MAY, 1910.]

A New Vista.
' I dined with Anson (the Warden of All Souls') last Sunday, and he recommended me to learn some modern history and come up *this* year (November), which is very perplexing and would be a terribly

Patrick Shaw-Stewart.

strenuous programme, as I should be quite certain to fail, and would then have to learn Law terribly swiftly to take the Jurisprudence School in June. But with the recommendation of the Warden I suppose one ought to be comparatively brave.'

[MAY 22, 1910.]

. . . . . .

Patrick got his first in Greats without any hesitation on the part of his examiners. He had not yet finished with 'work,' nor had he severed his connection with Oxford, since the All Souls' now lay in front of him, but as his undergraduate period ends here, it seems most appropriate to make this the starting-point of a new chapter.

Chapter Four

OF the next few years of Patrick's life I am far less competent to write, or even to select the extracts from his correspondence that will be the most characteristic or the most informing. I saw him, as a rule, when he came up to Oxford and stayed at All Souls', but the centre of his life now lay in London, which is farther removed from Oxford than an hour's journey on the Great Western would seem to indicate; and, tenacious as he was of old friendships, it was not possible but that his ever-widening ripple of acquaintance should attach new significance to it, which carried him beyond, without making him disloyal to older associations. It was not that the financial world into which his employment under Baring Brothers led him altered his outlook in any substantial way. It fascinated him, certainly, but chiefly as a toy fascinates a child; it pleased him, he said, to be in a place where you referred to eight thousands of pounds simply as 'eight.' But he was still adapting means to ends; finance was only a golden bridge to something, he was not quite sure what. His intellectual interests were, I think, stimulated by the feeling that the world of intellect was no longer composed of a series of examinations. He hated work, and the Classics lost the stigma of 'work' when Greats lay behind him. But other influences were forming

Patrick Shaw-Stewart.

him, more personal and less easy to calculate in the widening of his social horizon.

It will have been obvious to any one who has read thus far that he was already, while at Oxford, becoming a welcome guest in places where brilliance of conversation was prized and appreciated. Conscious that this was his only real asset, since he felt himself a sportsman only *pour rire* and held a low opinion of his personal appearance, he made it a sort of hobby to collect invitations, to find himself in new atmospheres, to succeed where failure might have been prophesied.

The natural outlet for his attainments was personal, not literary or public; he craved a theatre for his gifts, and lived delightedly in a turmoil of intellectual competition, in which he played the part of a soldier of fortune living by his rapier.

His difficulty in reconciling the claims of the office stool with those of the ball-room and of the distant week-end sometimes almost achieve the height of tragedy. Aided by a strong constitution and a huge energy of brain, he never seemed to let either suffer. But there is in all the letters of this period a note of apprenticeship, of a day coming when these irksome restrictions will no longer tie him down—as if he were still a school-boy, counting the days to the end of term—which adds to the bitterness of his premature loss. We are apt to find a special sense of tragedy about the death of those who went out fresh from school or University, whose careers were cut short *dulcis in limine vitæ*;

Patrick Shaw-Stewart.

but these at least had known life at its fullest, and only gave up life when they were compelled to give up fugitive youth; those who had laboriously and unwillingly built up the foundations of a career of which they were never to know the fruition leave behind them a more poignant record of wasted effort.

During the greater part of this next period Patrick is working at Bishopsgate, still linked to the past by occasional visits to All Souls', even after his 'year' of residence has expired, still keeping the future open for himself by flirtations with Law. And always when night sets him free from work, or Saturday gives him two days in the country, the relics of his time are jealously saved up for fresh experiences and fresh acquaintances. One or two foreign excursions diversify the story, especially his expedition to the United States (for purposes of business training) which comes to an end immediately before the war.

Prospects.

'You saw my letter about Barings, and there's not very much to add to that. It's practically decided now that I go there about the New Year, soon after All Souls' is over, and enter upon my clerkship and probation. So there it is, and I'm really very well satisfied with it. I've broken loose from London with a great effort, and leave to-day (after a culminating ball at the Duchess of Wellington's last night) for the long postponed reading

Patrick Shaw-Stewart.

party at dear old Brancaster. I shall stay there till just before the Viva, for which I shall probably go to Mells (and thence to Oxford and back), afterwards to Brancaster again, when the history Don will be there and will ask me questions, etc. I've had quite fun in London despite the problems, and I still retain my youthful appetite for balls. Sunday before last I spent at Esher, and last at Taplow, both elderly parties but most entertaining; Mr Balfour motored me down there on Saturday evening after the wonderful win of Eton at Lords, and we had a most thrilling conversation—mostly about Greek historians!' [JUNE 14, 1910.]

' Also I have to work more than you can possibly imagine, to do with all this history for All Souls' —I was a perfect mug ever to go in for it.' [AUGUST 18, 1910.]

' Just one word is all I can write, because I am in the miserable middle of All Souls'.
' (By the way, if you had any lingering hope or imagination about that institution, cut it out. I have done two hopeless papers, and have no prospect of doing any better ones.
' The thing is merely absurd: but of course you know that.) ' [OCTOBER 25, 1910.]

All Souls'.
' Here is a new address for you. I hope you will like it. I trust you got my telegram yesterday

Patrick Shaw-Stewart.

afternoon—I rather doubt it, because I gave it to a very seedy individual to send. It's an extraordinarily pleasant and fortunate thing this, distinctly the best that has ever happened to me, and so unexpected that I don't blame myself for the very gloomy accounts I gave—in fact I've lost £15 in bets against myself.' [NOVEMBER 4, 1910.]

'But I hear that the Sub-Warden said that the form of my papers was better than the matter—he well might. In general, I have heard much more of the previous inquiry into my morals (which appears to have been stringent and widespread, from Raymond's possibly rather lurid accounts) than of the exam. itself.' [NOVEMBER 7, 1910.]

'It's rather like being a fag at Eton again, especially for me, who am Junior Fellow or Screw, have to perform menial offices like making the salad, and decanting port wine (not so very unlike making toast and brewing tea): what I shall do with myself all this term I don't know—probably read French novels, or I might take one or two of the Bar exams.' [NOVEMBER 7, 1910.]

'I gather that some very odd things were said about me at the moral inquisition before the election, and from time to time I can see a Fellow looking at me with a wild eye as if he wasn't quite sure what I was going to do next.

Patrick Shaw-Stewart.

'I look particularly undesirable at present, as I got a rich black eye playing the wall game at Eton on Tuesday.' [NOVEMBER 10, 1910.]

A Contretemps.

'I finished Lockinge on Friday in great style, except for the hideous misfortune of breaking two vases the last night at billiard fives. It was too awful, and the confession before departing on Friday morning was a very throaty affair.'
[NOVEMBER, 1910.]

Diversions.

'There were several things last week, notably the Albert Hall ball on Wednesday, which I was ass enough to go to, although they didn't, I'm sorry to say, class me with Edward among the well-known young men. We dined for it before at the Sheffields in full dress. I made an effective entry, being late, clattering up the staircase in my sabots, with a blue blouse and *enormous* trousers and orange socks and a two-foot pipe and a worsted cap (and as the night wore on I scored heavily in my ideally comfortable clothes over the tired " gallants " in their ruffs and cloaks and swords and tight doublets). I got to bed *chez* Eddie at 6.30 a.m., and caught the 12.30 to Oxford, which I call not bad—rode a horse, and ran with the Toggers, and next day went to Marlborough to play racquets for Balliol against the school in place of Bill, who had a running match at Oxford and couldn't go. [MARCH 3, 1911.]

Patrick Shaw-Stewart.

'I get up for Chapels in order to practise for Bish. It's very near now, this is Thursday, and on Monday (Whit) I go to London, and on Tuesday morning I put on my little round black coat, my paper cuffs, and take the tube at Chancery Lane (D.V.) at about 9.15 a.m. It's a curious forward reflection, not wholly credible, but I suppose it will work itself out before my astonished gaze.'
[ALL SOULS', MAY, 1911.]

In the City.—To Lady Hermione Buxton.
'I am settling terribly well to the commercial collar. I believe the life was made for me—but more the life of a clerk than of a director.'
[JULY 3, 1911.]

.

'It's funny being at Barings. . . . I don't mind it much, hardly at all, but I am still quite bewildered. It's not very like anything I've done before—in fact it might be said to be very unlike; they are all very patient and explanatory.'
[JUNE 8, 1911.]

'*Are* we going to war? I wish you'd tell me; the times are so damned stirring. I shall join the C.I.V., I think—or is there an opening for naval volunteers devoid of any sort of qualification except good cross-Channel " stom "-powers?'
[JULY 27, 1911.]

Patrick Shaw-Stewart.

'What are your views on life, especially with regard to the immediate future? Mine are tinged with the deepest gloom, and I have been through a period of unwonted depression, with general discomfort, probably due to curtailed sleeping hours. Also reaction against happy disposition towards Barings. Also disgust at myself for inability to refrain from dancing, etc., every night till 3 a.m., which is, in the circumstances, neither amusing nor salubrious. [JULY 17, 1911.]

To his Sister.

'What a solemn thought that we have both increased our age. Undoubtedly such an addition has its graver as well as its gayer and more joyous side. This latter side was, however, nobly represented in my case, by the *immense* B.P.'s of W. and K. Their actual encashment went speedily in the way of what we here call "petty cash," but their equivalent credits could not, I think (do you?), be better employed than in contributing to my terribly Uncle Johnny kilt which has just got under way. What do you say to being half a sporran with K.? —or, if you're too proud for that, you could be a whole pair of tartan hose!—anyhow, there it is— it's going to be the most lovely old Stewart tartan, because the Royal is too red, and the Hunting is, you will agree, inappropriate to the polished floor.' [AUGUST 25, 1911.]

Patrick Shaw-Stewart.

'London isn't such a bad place as you think—really I like it better than anywhere, there is no beastly out of doors, and no cold and wet and exposure. It's a little empty at present tho'. I'm in a new department here, Commercial Credits, which I think is going to be rather entertaining.'
[OCTOBER 4, 1911.]

'Pity me; I am trying to pass Criminal Law on a week's work—and when I say a week's work, I mean evenings only—and when I say evenings, two of those were wasted by theatres. I am a perfect mug, and shall fail. Still, if I could just pass, it would be a delicious thing in its way—better than All Souls', better than Greats, though nobody would know it. But it's a curiously hard thing, which I never suspected before, to work in the evening to any purpose after " working " all day, even without any head-using.' [OCTOBER 7, 1911.]

'I am reading, which is something new these days. Zimmern's *Greek Commonwealth* and the *Oxford Book of Ballads* and Trevelyan's *Garibaldi* and Goschen's *Foreign Exchanges*—always an eye to the main chance, you see.' [OCTOBER 21, 1911.]

'I haven't much news of myself, the City, on the other hand, teeming with quiet fun; the six-power loan is almost through, but opinions divided as to whether they should wait for peace to issue or not. Then the Turks, poor creatures, are crying

Patrick Shaw-Stewart.

for money, and were on the point of getting some from the National Bank of Turkey and other members of an English, French, and German group, when yesterday's news came in—when once peace does get made there will be a most prodigious rush for new loans that ever was!' [JANUARY 24, 1912.]

' I've been working fairly hard—they've made me secretary to the English Committee of the Trans-Persian Ry. which Errington is running for us. That'll be a lot of interesting work and perhaps even a few halfpence. [MARCH 29, 1912.]

' But with reasonable luck there will be a stoppage for some time, or at worst another meeting to-morrow, which I could easily wait for. You see, at present, till they have fixed on the 8th member of the British group, I am a dummy director as well as Sec.—I can't very well miss either a meeting or the turbid period of correspondence. London was still dog-empty from Easter when I left it, but the truncated Taplow was a good little party. If all goes well I leave here for Rome to-morrow, stay there about a week and perhaps two days in Milan, and then back at the end of next week with quite a reasonable quantum of holidays still in my pocket for September. My violent moving in to Piccadilly has given place to a period of utter inertia, and I have no notion when my book-strewn floor will begin to be debarrassed. Now I must go and wrestle with the Haute Banque.' [PARIS, APRIL, 1912.]

Patrick Shaw-Stewart.

Italy Again.—To his Nurse.

'I have been meaning to write for a week, and say thank you frightfully for the lovely spoons, they are perfectly delightful, I do love them, and remember them well, but I wish you wouldn't do such a pelican when you are just setting up house on your own. It is too absurd, and you know you are much more likely to give tea parties than me—still you shall have tea with them when you come to London. Thank you ever so much, my own Dear. I had great luck about getting abroad just now, the first meeting of the English and French groups of the Trans-Persian was on Monday week, and the first of the whole Board is day after to-morrow, both in Paris, so there was just a comfortable ten days of Italy in between. I went straight to Rome, and had a lovely time with Charles, I couldn't live with him unfortunately, because he hadn't got a bed, but I lived *on* him persistently.'

[MAY 1, 1912.]

Managing Director.

'It's rather thrilling being a Managing Director, though the actual signature wears off slightly. My virgin document was a cheque for £100,000, which gave me an exquisite sensation, but since then I have to sign 500 Dividend warrants in 20 minutes, and wished I had taken one of the partners' advice and used " P. Stewart "! '

[FEBRUARY 13, 1913.]

Patrick Shaw-Stewart.
An Easter Holiday.
'I did get off Saturday though, which was more than Alan did, these poor Government's hacks! I played tennis at Brighton and rode magnificently on the Downs, and went late to bed, and rose later. I took twelve fat books with me, and read one short story. Altogether a fine Easter, and too soon over. I hope yours was fun—any Basil?'
[MARCH 27, 1913.]

Naples.
'Life here has been simplified by the presence of the Miller Mundy yacht in the harbour, which has taken us all with ease and grace to places like Pompeii and Pozzuoli—Pom is a good place for a popular *coup d'œil*, but I should have liked rather to have had a tame expert.' [APRIL 8, 1913.]

Rome and Pisa.
'It's sad going back, and yet there are, I suppose, compensations. I have no more money, and I'm tired of talking foreign languages, and I should like some poached eggs and bacon most frightfully, also I have a tooth asserting itself, and I trust none but home-grown dentists. It's been great fun of different kinds. I left Naples on Tuesday, and spent two nights in Rome again, including the far-famed Embassy ball, at which I alone out of 500 was not attired as a magnate with real pearls and real stuff, as worn by great-great-great. It was, as Charles said, not the ball to go to as a postage stamp; and

Patrick Shaw-Stewart.

yet I braved it as a fisherman of Sorrento, there being no further resources in the one Neapolitan Costumier. Luckily they are dressy chaps, the Sorrentine fishermen, the greater part of their costume being exactly like court-dress, and anyhow, I wasn't turned out. Of course the " Eyetalians " looked very splendid, but we've seen all that *so* often at the Albert Hall. Well, well, I shall be able to tell my grandchildren about it—my invariable excuse for these follies—they will get very confused in their minds about fancy balls, poor mites. The day after, I took Charles off to Pisa, where we have been meditating for two days of the vanity of human endeavour, and the abuses of the modern state; all this from Charles's new standpoint of crusted (though fiercely enlightened) Toryism. It is a jolly place, quite silent and lovely, with four well-defined sights, which you can learn by heart, within a cricket pitch of each other.'

[APRIL, 1913.]

Venice.

' Venice is incredibly like what I had been brought up to expect it traditionally and pictorially —and particularly like the representation at Earl's Court last year; none the less attractive for that: one's life threatened daily by the dank surroundings in the town, and daily restored by lawn-tennis and bathing at the Lido. (This excellent institution, reached in ten minutes by our host's tigsy steam-launch, is what really eats in to the time for

Patrick Shaw-Stewart.

sightseeing.) Looking back, I wonder that I ever got inside S. Mark's: but I did—just—and also into one or two other agreeable and notorious places.

Edward was there, in magnificent form, as you may imagine: Venice is the perfect setting for him—and several other congenial youths. I am travelling back with Evan Charteris, who regarded us all with perpetual mild amazement.'

[OCTOBER 22, 1913.]

Saturday to Monday.
' I have been virtuous to All Souls'—this'll be my 3rd Sunday there running, but as it'll be followed by a Taplow, a Belvoir, and two Grimthorpes, perhaps it's as well to acquire a little merit early in the term.' [NOVEMBER 7, 1913.]

Prospects of American Travel.
' To-night is the far-famed Picture Ball: I—as you may have gathered from the dailies or the weeklies—forming part of a group representing the birth of futurism, in which my garments are very peculiar, and my sex (to say the least of it) indeterminate, as I wear a skirt (white satin with blobs of various colours) and carry a symbolic infant in my arms. This is really to say that it seems not improbable I may be sent to America (New York and Boston) soonish for about six months. This between you and me; it may come to nothing or it may be postponed, but I think it'll be pretty soon—I don't

Patrick Shaw-Stewart.

know whether I like it or not : I shall probably loathe it when I'm there: but it's a change certainly: and if it's accompanied by a Rise, it may be faced with equanimity. I'll write again about it.'
[DECEMBER 3, 1913.]

The Voyage.—To Lady Hermione Buxton.

'Among other joys of the voyage has been that I have not known *one soul* on board, nor have attempted to know one; you probably mark that against me as unsociable, as well as foolish, in not extending my net; but you don't know (*a*) how really shy I am; (*b*) what my arrears in general reading were. (Also I wanted to know if any one would madly cultivate me for my looks alone; but my serviceable face has stood the test; not one fellow-passenger has made the attempt.) Do you know any useful facts about America?

'Tell me if you do, and be indiscreet at the distance of 2500 miles. That's why I write, you say: all right—but do.' [JANUARY 31, 1914.]

To his Sister.

'It's been very jolly, I do love the sea; quite warm, so that I could sit on deck a lot; and bed from 11 p.m. to 12 noon, so I'm a new creature.

'I've not known *one* soul on board, thank God! such a collection of funnies and frumps, you never did see. I did have a moment's regret when the C's didn't turn up as advertised, but on calm

Patrick Shaw-Stewart.

reflection I doubt if even Lady C. would have been worth my peace. The first night at dinner I sat next an aged gentleman, who told me that two acres had been added to the British Empire every second during the 19th century. "Every time the clock went like *that*," he added, with a sawing motion of the hand. I thought that if it was a question of fifteen meals with a statistician I might be pardoned for violent measures: so next day at luncheon I asked for a table alone, and my fifteen meals have been consumed in solitary grandeur, as indeed has every minute of my eight days.

'Such fun; and the things I've read! *Rhoda Fleming*, *Père Goriot*, *An Agnostic's Apology*, and *Clare on the Money Market*, not to speak of the *Odyssey* and the *Oxford Book of E.V.* And I've learnt to smoke a pipe again, and my soul has grown yards. I can't describe to you what the attentions of the Cunard Co. to Barings emissary have been, but I enclose the menu of one of my "special little dinners" to give you a faint idea. (The head waiter always orders one for me at eight, having had an instinctive—and right—feeling from the first that seven wouldn't suit me.) The band even asked me what I would like my food played down with; but, not feeling sure whether the Liebestod or Yip-i-addy would strike the more congenial note, I gave it up.

'What it'll all cost in tips, ah me!'

[FEBRUARY 1, 1914.]

Patrick Shaw-Stewart.

The People.

'Their hours are fairly stiff here, one's thought very lordly if one's later than 9.30 in the morning —however, I've not had many temptations so far to be late at night, so I'm getting very plump and rosy. Mrs Astor, who would have been my stand-by in this City, has " gone to Europe," which is very sad, but there are one or two others to fall back on. Next week I go over to Boston for two or three days, to say " How do you do" to the partners there —and then back here for two or three months solid. The people here are very sweet and almost too courtly in their attitude, they don't appear to want me to do any work at all. I hope to move out of my hotel soon, as it's damned expensive: I have a small body of efficient but varied people, including J. Pierpont Morgan junior, on the look-out for a suitable apartment for a poor but honest young man, but nothing has come of it yet.

[NEW YORK, FEBRUARY 6.]

The Climate.

'This is the coldest day they have had in Boston for eighteen years, and this morning it was fourteen below zero. I didn't feel much of it myself, as I took a taxi from door to door on excellent advice, but when I opened my mouth to tell the taxi man where to go to, I found I was unable to articulate, as the full force of the fourteen below zero had just entered my diaphragm. It's a curious feeling but rather exhilarating, one of the odd parts of it is, that

Patrick Shaw-Stewart.

if you have a slight catarrh, your nose gets *internally* frozen as soon as you get out of doors, a most remarkable sensation. (I came here day before yesterday, and the cold snap arrived almost simultaneously). Of course it's quite *dry* cold, no damp in the bones; but the wind, all the same, makes you feel as if you had swallowed an ice too quick the whole time you're out of doors.'

[BOSTON, FEBRUARY 12.]

The Jolly People.

' I've made friends with several very jolly people, who seem to form a more or less composite whole, which is a great thing when you're only staying a short time in a place, as you don't have to meet a dozen new people every time you dine out. For really the trial of remembering these people's faces and their names is a perfect nightmare; and, as you know, though fair at names, I'm real bad at faces—so I just have to go about in public with a fixed, idiotic smile which'll do for any one.'

[MARCH 11.]

The Language.

' I am looked after by Japanese boys, who (after one has surmounted the first racial twinge) are quite good, and one of them, for a dollar a week, tries to fulfil the duties of Vidgen with my clothes; but it is weary work explaining to an alien who talks indifferent English and American-English at that, so that he refers to a dinner-jacket as a " Tuxedo," and drawers as "under-trousers," and inverts the use of the words "suspenders" and "braces."

'In language, the things to be careful of are, to say "Bawston" and "Shikawgo," to make great use of "right here" and "right now" (on asking if a lady were at home I have been deposited in the drawing-room with the words, "She'll be right down"), and to know the answer to "I'm vurry pleased to meet you, Mr Stoo'rt," or else to be very nippy and get it in first. (I really don't know the answer yet, though I've found that "not at all" isn't right.) The "clerks" (pronounce phonetically) say "I guess," but the 400 don't: on the other hand, the latter *do* say not only "gotten" but also "bully," which always makes me smile even now: and if one says "jolly" in the vague English way, one's got to be prepared to explain it—*e.g.* I used it of a particularly doleful book, meaning that I thought it a good piece of work. I'm getting good at saying, "I'll fix that up," and don't you think "having a crush on some one" a fine phrase for being slightly gone on her? Also "highbrows" is the only possible word for the Intellectuals (I am warned I shall see a lot of them in Boston). I love New York, and wish I was going to be here all the time—however, Newport is within two hours of Boston, and I have already raised two invitations for it, so I hope to solace the sultry summer months and not lose all the jollies I have been acquiring.'

[NEW YORK, MARCH 26.]

Patrick Shaw-Stewart.
Easter Monday.

'Observe the kind of day we bank on here; if Abraham Lincoln had resurrected they'd have had three holidays.

'I sent off a cable very ingloriously on Thursday night, but afterwards had qualms, arising out of the coincidence of a certain austere anniversary with your birthday: but afterwards I decided that good Scottish postmasters do *not* go to the 3-hour service. Personally I celebrated that evening by going to the opera with dear Mrs ———, who said she felt it was rather wicked, but at the same time she did not see why she should sit at home all the evening with her box wasting there, and she thought it would be all right if she wore black—(I wondered if I was expected to wear a black waistcoat).

'Two good headlines in my evening paper yesterday—one technically called the "Scarehead," about the four "gunmen" who are going to be executed for the Rosenthal murder two years ago. (You remember, the "Police—Lieut. Becker" case)—like this :—

GUNMEN ABANDON HOPE:
TURN TO RELIGION

the other a modest violet in a low corner explaining itself :—

HAD 3 WIVES; GETS 6 MONTHS

Patrick Shaw-Stewart.

'Some one wrote to me as "dear Patrick" the other day—I have seen her *once*. In this country they call that "nerve" (and pronounce it "noive," which makes it sound worse).'

[APRIL 13.]

Washington.

'They don't go in for any unnecessary reticences here. They are both terse and vigorous—I've just asked the man in the office about steamers on the Mississippi, and he said, " No, *Sir*! them dog-gone boats haven't started yet, it's been too damned cold——" Not that I really *mind* the language, you understand, but it's so surprising to be treated so intimately. I left New York with many regrets 6 days ago, on Monday, and went to Washington, where I stayed 3 nights with Eustace Percy.

'Washington is a fine city, and a great relief to the eye after New York, as there is room there to build the houses low and have trees and things about. The population to the casual eye seems about half nigger—really, I believe it's about a quarter. The first day I was there it was 96° in the shade, the second about 66°—the change had the surprising effect of curing an incipient cold in me. I saw the Capitol (and listened to speeches in *both* grimy little Chambers) and the Congressional Library (" finest building in de world, sah! " said my nigger driver, who really did say it like that), and the Smithsonian Park and the River Potómac (mind the accent), and the Pan-American building,

Patrick Shaw-Stewart.
which is superb. I also observed the British Embassy at work and at play.' [MAY 17, 1914.]

On Tour.
 ' I believe you'd like Arizona: it's stretching out for endless miles on both sides of me just now, just sand and alkali (whatever that is) and sage and scrub, interminably dotted with pale sandstone rocks. A good deal of the sand (and Alkali) is in my throat and all down my œsophagus, and my tongue is hanging out and my head throbs, and I long for the flesh-pots of Los Angeles: but before that I am heroically " stopping off " a day to see the Grand Canyon, the wonder of the world, which I kind of suspect is going to bore me. Now I am crossing the Continent, which Baring Brothers think will broaden my mind—let us hope so. Then two months in Boston, and then, by the grace of God, England. And yet I am not homesick. I've really " got a crush," as they say, on this bustling, simple-minded, gaseous, rather incompetent, hospitable nation.' [MAY 21, 1914.]

To his Nurse.
 ' I went from St Louis up to Keokuk in Iowa where the great dam over the Mississippi is (I was shown that all one morning, and a fat lot I understood about it), and from there to Quiney (Illinois) and Kansas City, where the Santa Fe railroad starts and takes you right out to the Pacific at Los Angeles

Patrick Shaw-Stewart.

—three days' solid journey, except for a day I broke the journey at the Grand Canyon, and was fool enough to go down it—nothing but dust and hot draughts, you *see* much better from outside. It's an overrated old place anyhow, *I* think, just an inverted mountain with a dirty mill race at the bottom. Los Angeles is a pretty town, with lovely avenues of palm and gum-trees, and groves of oranges and grape-fruits—it is also the most self-advertising town I have yet met in this country, and that's saying a good deal. The " boosters " or town advertisers there are a regular profession, and they shout at you from every placard. I was so enthusiastic about the Pacific Ocean that I went to a " resort " called Venice near there and bathed in the surf—very cold but romantic. From there I went to San Francisco (see my next), and am now on my way to the Old Flag at Vancouver, and I can tell *you*, Dear, I shall soon have had enough travelling to last me the rest of my natural.'

[MAY 30.]

' Nothing like being on British soil. The Empire, you know, and all that—very inspiring, and a better climate, too, than in most parts of those United States. San Francisco, now, I thought that was going to be an agreeable place, but in the evening a cold gray fog came up out of the Pacific and a fierce wind accompanied it and shivered my semi-tropical timbers. It's a fine place to look at, certainly, especially from up above, and the 1915 Exhibition

Patrick Shaw-Stewart.

Buildings, which are nearly finished now, are lovely (Romano-byzantino-arabesque, I should say), and the food in the restaurants is good. But from the human point of view I was sadly put out by a deceptive woman. She told me there was no one worth knowing in San Francisco or Los Angeles she wouldn't put at my disposal. So I didn't take any trouble about those places with any one else—then she never did. It's a shy-making business at best, walking briskly round with a pocketful of letters of introduction and standing twirling your hat while the recipients digest them: but, as I've now found from experience, it's shyer and sadder still to be in a large new city without them. Some brazen people, I believe, send them on ahead, but I've never quite dared to do that.

'From San Francisco onwards I began to realise that there are distances North and South in this continent as well as East and West. It took me two nights and a day to get to Portland, which I had imagined to be next door. There I spent a hot day among the roses with the British Consul. From there to Seattle was one night (my 10th in the train!) and Seattle to Vancouver one day, the latter by boat, a lovely day's sail, even to the travellers surfeited with North American scenery. I got here about 8 on Sunday and was mildly surprised to find it still light for nearly an hour—the simple fact being that I've come the best part of 2000 miles due north in the last week.

[VANCOUVER, JUNE 2.]

Patrick Shaw-Stewart.

'We went through the Rockies, which were in excellent form, travelling by day, and then over the foot-hills and beginnings of the prairie to Calgary, where they have just struck oil and are all as mad as hatters about it: there's really only about a gallon of oil as yet, I believe, but they have samples of oil in bottles in all the shop windows, and lists of oil shares up on slates outside, like "Special Dishes to-day." Thus one sees the primitive embryo of the Stock Exchange! Then we changed and went north to Edmonton, which is the gate of all the Great North-West centre of the northern wheat country, and depot for all the fur-trade. Not a bad country, but a *filthy* hotel, where there was dry-rot: and yet, when we got to Winnipeg, and into a really sumptuous Ritz-like affair,——had the ingratitude to do nothing but bemoan the improvidence of building such an hotel in such a place, and gloomily repeat that some one told him the management lost 1000 dollars a day on it.' [JUNE 18.]

A Valediction.

'All the same, it's strange but true that I shall be sorry in some ways to see the last of the Statue of Liberty. I've got acclimatised to this country, and the drinks are so good, and the people so jolly (and so fond of the English!), and Newport is such a magnificent place, and I am just slightly in love

Patrick Shaw-Stewart.

with a very tall, very thin lady with scarlet hair and slanting eyes who beats me at lawn tennis.'

[JUNE 25, 1914.]

. . . . . .

It will be seen that the end of the American visit almost coincided with the outbreak of war; the rest of Patrick's time at Bishopsgate belongs, therefore, to the next chapter.

Chapter Five

THE extracts I have given in this chapter will explain themselves without even the need of distinguishing headlines. The outbreak of war found Patrick at Bishopsgate; he had, as the reader of the earlier chapters will easily divine, no tenderness for Pacificist doctrines, and he was sufficiently in touch with the gossip, whether of the City or of Whitehall, to realise at once something of the magnitude of those labours which lay before us. All August he remained at his office-stool, dealing with a situation unfamiliar even to the most experienced of financiers; in September he obtained leave to devote himself to the fortunes of war, and looked about, as most people who had any influence did at that time, for some appointment which would bring him as quickly as possible near the scene of operations. He knew the ropes of Whitehall as well as most people; and only a few days after his application had been made, was offered and accepted a position as interpreter to the naval forces which, with the 7th Division, were sent out to Belgium in a desperate attempt to outflank or at least to check the German advance from the North. He remained at Dunkirk during the last few days of September and most of October, finding, as was the experience of many others, that a job which could be found for a civilian to do without any of the delays of

Patrick Shaw-Stewart.

military training was not likely to be a job which threatened honourable scars. He returned to England at the end of October, and, already committed to the older of the two Services, threw in his lot with the Naval Division, then in training at the Crystal Palace. This centre had not then the unenviable medical reputation it afterwards acquired, and Patrick easily made himself happy there by availing himself of the frequent opportunities for going up to London and dining where he would. His evenings, probably, were hardly less crowded now than when his days were tied to Bishopsgate.

The transference of the Division to Blandford for Field Training was to him something of an exile. But, at the same time, he obviously begins to be more bitten with his job, and the platoon of stokers suffering a land-change into combatants is a problem clearly attractive to him. Yet, inasmuch as all field training has its samenesses, and the total amount of letters dating from this period is not large, I have thought it best to make this chapter short, reserving for a later one the cruise on the *Grantully Castle*, during which, it would seem, that close Freemasonry between the remarkable officers of the present *Hood* Battalion first came into existence. The set of extracts, then, only carries us down to the sailing of the Naval Division in February, 1915.

. . . . .

' It seems this morning that war is quite inevitable. Hardly credible, is it ? Also, though this is private

Patrick Shaw-Stewart.

at present (it won't be when it reaches you), the Bank have authority to suspend the Bank Act: that is, to issue more bank notes against securities, *not against gold*. The result of that if put into operation will inevitably be the suspension of specie payments, and the result of *that* possibly a general " moratorium " or suspension of debts. Not that you and I, as private and extremely small individuals, need worry: some machinery will be invented for daily needs, the banks will keep faith, and they and the Bank are working together. . . . The Stock Exchange is closed; they couldn't stand the flood of Continental selling orders. " Nothing stands that stood before." But all the banks happen to be in a particularly strong position, especially Baring Brothers: only we must stop the flow of gold out of the country somehow, as no payments are coming in from abroad.

'The Americans have shipped vast quantities of gold, but I don't think they can do much more. They are pretty uncomfortable themselves now, and have closed the New York Exchange.

'All this sounds more alarming than perhaps it need be: the simple fact is that, while there is no panic in London and no one is " talked about " or in a weak position, yet the entire existing machinery of credit is unequal to the international situation, and something new has got to be devised to carry us along. At present your money is *perfectly* safe in Coutts's!

Patrick Shaw-Stewart.

' I am thinking of joining the London Scottish! I think they will probably be made to do something honourable and *safe*, and the kilt is so becoming.'
[AUGUST 1, 1914.]

' These are strange days: I've got a brother just off or just going from Ireland—and, ludicrous fact! my own unwarlike soul is so disturbed that I have gone as far as to apply for information about the Inns of Court O.T.C. A pretty soldier I should make! But I don't fancy I shall ever get to the Low Countries.' [AUGUST 5, 1914.]

' It's exciting enough in the City, God knows, with the whole world going on a paper currency, and every one owing every one else money (which there is no means of paying) at a bank rate of ten per cent.' [AUGUST 5, 1914.]

' The City is outwardly quiet, and the *currency* question is settled—for the time, anyhow; but the *credit* difficulty will yet have to be settled, and every one here is cudgeling his brains over it. The main difficulty, in two words, is to prop up those big houses who have debts owing from Germany which will never be paid, and, if they go under, to prevent the whole City coming down like a pack of cards on the top of them. This applies (a) to banks; (b) more or less in parallel form to the Stock Exchange. I may seem to be speaking sensationally, and don't repeat this, because the public (mercifully) think

Patrick Shaw-Stewart.

all is well now that it's got its notes: but if you saw the length of the faces of those who know, you would realise this is one of the most terrific things London has been up against since finance existed. The remedy will undoubtedly take the form of the Government shouldering the whole thing.'
[AUGUST 21, 1914.]

' In spite of ——, a kind of involuntary and grumbling militarism is beginning to reassert itself, to my great discomfort, in my interior. Now what would you two say if I could find some nice safe method of spending an open-air life with the consent of my employers for the next few months? Say an O.T.C.—or Superintendent of Stores at Portsmouth—or Interpreter at Havre—or Chaplain—or Genealogist to determine Questions of Precedence in the Indian Army? You see, really, when all is said and done, I am not the actual pivot of the city's financial life, and eight people have been known at a pinch to do the work of nine—did, indeed, when I was in America. Let me know your views, but don't strain anything over it. I shall probably make up my own so-called mind eventually, after the machinery has sufficiently creaked.'
[SEPTEMBER 10, 1914.]

' I suppose to settle things in rather perplexing circumstances is good practice for a financier—and, talking of financiers, Baring Brothers have been perfect angels, and given me their blessing, their

Patrick Shaw-Stewart.

promise to keep my place warm, and half-pay. Better practice still, perhaps, is taking decisions quickly; and, that, also, I have accomplished in the last twenty-four hours. After a week of language cramming, and three days catching cold in the passages of the War Office, I have been offered, and accepted, a post as interpreter, to fulfil which I am to go abroad as soon as I can get my equipment. I know nothing about all the questions of horse, servant, baggage, arms (! l), and all the ridiculous questions one asks. . . .

' The force I am going with, and its mission, are rather odd and a dead secret (which makes it all the more thrilling to the mind well educated on *Chums* and R.K.). They said I might tell you, so to speak, under seal, so I enclose a slip giving the facts. . . . Remember always that interpreters are practically non-combatants.'

(*Enclosed under separate cover.*) ' To Dunkirk to join a Marine Brigade and the Oxfordshire Yeomanry. (They went last night.) The commission would be as a Sub-lieutenant in the R.N.V.R. (a sailor-boy—think of it!) ' [SEPTEMBER 20, 1914.]

To His Nurse.
' I may have done completely wrong: but on the whole it seemed to me that what I have done was the only tolerable course, though by no means an attractive or a glamorous one. My own Dear, wherever a man spends his life these next months it is bound to be dreary and damnable: and with

Patrick Shaw-Stewart.

that fact well in mind I have decided on what seems to me the lesser 'evil. Now, in the last twenty-four hours I have been offered and accepted a post as interpreter, which—if it goes through smoothly—will mean my leaving in about five days. I wish I could dash up to see you and them before I go, but in the time it's impossible. I shall be dashing about every minute getting things, also I must be inoculated for typhoid.'   [SEPTEMBER 20, 1914.]

'Never have I spent a queerer day than yesterday. It started at 6 (significant, I dare say, of the future), and the portion of it before 8.30 when I left Little Grosvenor Street was, as you can imagine, fairly brisk. Of course, the back of the packing had been broken with great efficiency by K. overnight, but the remainder gave some food for thought in the morning. My resemblance to the White Knight when I staggered into my taxi was exact.

'We left Dover about 1 o'clock, and got into Dunkirk (after being twice stopped and questioned) about 6, but we didn't get ashore till 7. The town is very full, and there was some difficulty about billeting us—indeed, I haven't been officially billeted yet. We had an excellent dinner here, and I began my interpretations unofficially by taking some of our party to find beds elsewhere. Mercifully every one here seems to speak excellent French without an accent: a good many of the names are Flemish, and I suppose in the country one might be up against it. Eventually I got half a bed with one

Patrick Shaw-Stewart.

of the consul's new military assistants, a Balliol man who went down the year I went up. I was pretty tired, and slept through his going to bed beside me; on the other hand he says I jabbed him sharply in the stomach about 4 a.m. This morning we retrieved our kit from the ship, I have since reported myself to the General, the Brigade-Major, the Intelligence Department, the latter I have got to keep on doing till they have time to see me.'
[DUNKIRK, SEPTEMBER 27, 1914.]

To His Nurse.
' I was kept dangling all yesterday, as well as all Sunday, as the Yeomanry had been thoughtless enough to procure a Frenchman to interpret. Then, late last night, they told me I was to be Embarkation (or rather Dis-) Officer, which, as far as I can make out, means standing on the quay and saying " mind the gangway," and " all landing tickets, please."
' To that end I am to report this morning to one Colonel—who disputes with several other worthy Colonels here the honours of Base Commandant. Some things here seem to be very much under-manned, and one ought easily to find a sphere of activity: others again, more picturesque and dignified, are filled several times over, mostly by eminent amateurs.' [SEPTEMBER 29, 1914.]

To His Nurse.
' I have been nearly a fortnight in France now, and no nearer the old front than when I landed. My

Patrick Shaw-Stewart.

sword, revolver, and wire-cutters are honourably rusting; my Wolseley valise and waterproof sheet are laid by in cold storage, while I use my silk pyjamas, and the elegant bedstead of a Dunkirk grain merchant, who has gone to the front, and whose anxious lady finds her only relaxation in providing for my comfort. It is not wildly exciting being Embarkation Officer: on the other hand, it might easily be much worse, and wants a lot of looking after. Of course, our position here as a base of supplies, and generally our aim in life, may be enormously modified in the next few days by what happens at some considerable distance away, so for the moment everything is pretty temporary; but as long as there is anything to embark or disembark there must be ME. The people here are very jolly on the whole, though not supremely congenial; there is a fair sprinkling of amateurs of whom most are Radical M.P.'s. Altogether, it's a comfortable kind of way of being at war. Own Dear, it was sweet of you to come to London, and it was lovely seeing you. I should never have got off without you three to get the things for me.'

[DUNKIRK, OCTOBER 9, 1914.]

To Lady Desborough.
 ' I am still Embarkation Officer, and have been now for a fortnight. I suppose one might be doing far drearier things, and obviously one could hardly have been doing a less uncomfortable thing. The only feeling of slight mutinousness in the back of

Patrick Shaw-Stewart.
my mind arises from the reasoning which I can't quite get rid of, that I did want either (a) a dash or (b) some solid military training: and it looks as if I was going to get neither. And having left Bishopsgate on the ground that by age and fitness I could stand a campaign, it seems rather silly to be doing work that any ex-Colonel of seventy could do. I must say it's frightfully absorbing to the civilian eye to see the workings of even the hindermost tail-end of an army, the nature and attitude of the parts and their relation to the whole. Very queer indeed: I shall write a book about it one of these days.'
[OCTOBER 13, 1914.]

'The fall of Antwerp is bound to affect all the arrangements in this part of the world fairly considerably. Conceivably, I might find the base of which I form part sent trundling across the Channel: in which case there would be nothing for it but to pin a large medal across my chest and join the New Army. On the other hand, things may continue as they are, or even if the " base " disappears I may get transferred and stay on here. Anyhow, there seems no prospect of my going farther afield than this. I will write as soon as I know.

'It has not been uninteresting here altogether, though rather monotonous (but then I am well broken in to office life), and a little depressing owing to the misfortunes of Antwerp and the Naval Division. There will probably be a good deal of subterraneous criticism of the sending of the British

Patrick Shaw-Stewart.

detachment—on the other hand, if Antwerp hadn't fallen, it would have been acclaimed as an inspiration.

'I, personally, when I am not prostrated before the Base Commandant, am mostly taking orders from the Naval Embarkation Officer, who, though theoretically co-equal with me, is actually a Captain R.N., and very reverend. For the first week he was a sweet, rotund old thing to whom I was affectionate and winning, since then it has been a lean and rigorous martinet whose one delight is to find fault with the amateur. I lick his boots and execute all orders at the double.'

[DUNKIRK, OCTOBER 13, 1914.]

'It's an amusing life and very healthy (or would be, if I hadn't formed the habit of dining in London and taking the last suburban train back). The adjutant here was a ranker; he does most of the instructing, and puts the fear of God into us all. It is so funny after all one's academical and financial eminence to stand shivering in a row while he approaches like a witch-finder before you know which is the victim. It was me the other day; he said I was marching like a Chelsea Pensioner. At the end of it I shall certainly know how to " tell them off." '

[CRYSTAL PALACE, NOVEMBER 13, 1914.]

'I passed the examination at the end of my fortnight's Instruction Class (that is, at the end of last week), with some, but not too much, *éclat*, obtaining 78 marks out of 100. It was an anxious moment,

Patrick Shaw-Stewart.

because I had not devoted much of my evenings to preparation, and indeed, had to rely exclusively on my ancient faculty of deceiving the examiners. On Monday, then, I emerged into the "Depot Battalion" with the understanding that as soon as possible I shall be shunted into " Hood " Battalion, in the 2nd Brigade, where Ock Asquith, Rupert Brooke, the poet, and other niceish men now are.

'Meanwhile, comically enough, owing to the fact that all the Company Commanders are going through an Advanced Class, I find myself second in command of " A " Company of the Depot Battalion: so I may now be seen any day doubling about the parade ground, furtively consulting my *Infantry Training* in my pocket, trying to make 220 men hear my thin reedy tones, or explaining the mechanism of the rifle (a subject which I very imperfectly comprehend) to a whole platoon at a time. The situation is complicated by there being no subalterns *at all*; just me and a Company Commander as youthful and inexperienced as, though slightly more intelligent than, myself, to deal with this vast horde of men. The men, by the way, are Scottish to a man—from Buckie, Aberdeen, the Clyde—and are alarmingly intelligent, though not exactly smart.' [NOVEMBER 25, 1914.]

'Thank you for sweet letter, also for sheet, or rather converted sheet-bag, which works *admirably*, if one is intelligent about getting in and out shaped like a short, stout shoe-horn. . . .

Patrick Shaw-Stewart.

'Road-making consists of walking up and down a wide slab of liquid mud, between two rows of huts, waiting for one fatigue-party to bring stones in buckets from one quarter of the compass, and another to bring whins to put under them from the opposite quarter. The stones and the whins between them form the road, as the term is understood in our primitive circles. When the men bring them you graciously indicate with your toe where they should go, and say " Smartly there " and " double off now." That is road-making, and very chilly it is.'
[BLANDFORD, JANUARY 4, 1915.]

'The present routine is a curious contrast to the Crystal Palace, which was mostly explaining the parts of the rifle to admiring Scotchmen. In other ways also it's a curious contrast; my hut makes Mowbray Road, Upper Norwood, seem in retrospect like the palace of Sardanapalus. I don't mind it really, it makes me laugh when I contemplate my sleeping-quarters. Also the distance from London, oh dear, oh dear, that is a grim affair.'
[JANUARY 4, 1915.]

'. . . But as we say in the Navy, as long as you form a habit it doesn't very much matter what it is. It is almost incredible how one becomes assimilated to any new form of existence nowadays; Christmas seems like a bright vision, the Crystal Palace a distant memory, Dunkirk a previous existence, and anything before that a tale told by an idiot.'
[JANUARY 15, 1915.]

Patrick Shaw-Stewart.

'I have got the queerest command—imagine it —a platoon of Old Stokers! They are very queer fish to handle after the lamb-like Scots at the Crystal Palace—their appearance is rather like the *Punch* pictures of the Landsturm, their language extremely fruity, and their cunning almost inexhaustible. But (as you used to say about Pupshy) they have great "character," and I dare say they may grow on me. But they have got a sort of standing grievance in the back of their evil old minds that they want to be back in their steel-walled pen, yelping delight and rolling in the waist, instead of forming fours under the orders of an insolent young landlubber.' [JANUARY 15, 1915.]

'I have been marching literally 15 miles a day for all the last week bar two days, and once 20, and once 18, so I am, if possible, more in the pink of condition than ever, and very proud of the condition of my feet. The stokers on the other hand have very many blisters, poor souls, and complain bitterly that they aren't on the nice comfy sea. Meanwhile, two battalions of the Marine Brigade have been served out with pith helmets, and, as you may imagine, the result is that the air is thick with rumours— Egypt, E. Africa, S.-W. Africa, Cameroons, Persian Gulf, all freely mentioned, and any space of time from a week to three months; but I keep on believing nothing. (I must say, between you and me, I shouldn't exactly *mind* Egypt: so nice to see Cheops' Pyramid at your country's expense: and

Patrick Shaw-Stewart.

then the climate, such an improvement on Flanders in March.)

'Oh, by the way, the buzzing received an impetus yesterday when the C.O. solemnly made us practise forming square! It may have been only to puzzle the poor stokers (who did it very badly), but it seemed so very suggestive of Fuzzy-wuzzies or other crude foes. Personally I liked it: it seems to me the only form of modern warfare that gives the poor officers a chance.' [FEBRUARY 4, 1915.]

'For the last week we have been on a "billeting march" through the New Forest and thereabouts; Ringwood, Lyndhurst, Fordingbridge, about 15 and 18 miles a day. Then we were to have marched home on Friday, but we were stopped because some recruits from the Crystal Palace had got spotted fever, so we marched back to Ringwood and stayed there till this morning and marched back to-day. (Ringwood suited me very well, because the Manners' at Avon were quite close, and I took meals and bath salts off them.) I think we should have stayed away still longer, only we are to be inspected by Winston day after to-morrow, and must practise it to-morrow.'

[FEBRUARY 15, 1915.]

'Devitt said I ought to stay properly in bed three days, and stay in London till the end of the week (this week). None so pleased as me, and obediently I took to my bed; and it was in my bed on Monday

Patrick Shaw-Stewart.

morning that I got a telegram (of Saturday, overdue) from the Adjutant saying " warned for foreign service next week " (meaning this week), so I had to do a little fussing, I can tell you. I guessed pretty well at once what it was, but wormed it out of ———. to make sure. It is the Dardanelles, the real plum of this war: all the glory of a European campaign (and greater glory than any since Napoleon's, if we take Constantinople and avenge the Byzantine Empire), without the wet, mud, misery, and certain death of Flanders. Really I think we are very lucky and ——— an angel to have got it for us. We are supposed to sail on Saturday, our base is Lemnos—a fortnight's sea voyage, the most delicious thing in the world, and the best for my throat. Not a word about that base, by the way, nor for that matter about the campaign in general, unless it becomes obviously public property—most of all, don't say which day we sail or we shall be submarined for a certainty. I am really very pleased, and so ought you to be. It is the luckiest thing and the most romantic. Think of fighting in the Chersonese (hope you got the allusion from the Isles of Greece about Miltiades), or alternatively, if it's the Asiatic side they want us on, on the plains of Troy itself! I am going to take my Herodotus as a guide-book.'

[FEBRUARY 24, 1915.]

Chapter Six

It is a mark of the magic ship in the fairy story, whether it be Jason's Argo or the Flying Ship of Northern legend, that its crew should be all people of marked individual powers, a Ministry of all the Talents on the high seas. One must be the strong man, one the swift runner, one the archer of the party; Lynceus with his keen eyes, Mopsus the seer, and their fellows. There is something of this character about the sailing of the Naval Division, and of the Hood Battalion in particular. To mention no others, you get a fine grounding for a mess-room with Rupert Brooke the poet, Denis Browne the musician, Charles Lister, the humanitarian turned diplomat, and Patrick himself, the humanist turned financier. By a fated course, they even followed in the Argo's track, and delayed as Jason delayed at Lemnos; they proved anew the accuracy of that forgotten Greek sailor who christened the Dardanelles 'The Clashing Rocks,' so tempting a channel till you were within near distance, then impassable, bristling with death. And if our voyagers never penetrated the Symplegades and saw the Euxine open into view; if they came away apparently empty-handed, leaving only a tradition and a series of undying names, they did not in truth fail in their quest, or lose in death the recapture of the Golden Fleece they coveted—the honour of Belgium.

Patrick Shaw-Stewart.

Patrick's own descriptions of this part of his experience are warmly tinged with classical reminiscence. He had some classical books with him; the *Iliad* presumably, certainly Herodotus. Without a trace of antiquarian grimness or Baedekerian on-the-spot-ness he co-ordinates his impressions with the reading of his schooldays, partly no doubt from the books, but mostly from his amazing memory. After all, the country he was going to was the scene of the campaign about which he probably knew more details than about any other in history (if history it be); he was prepared to greet the plains of Troy as a *habitué*:—

'. . . Hic sævus tendebat Achilles,
Classibus hic locus, hic acie certare solebant.'

For the benefit of those who still do not despise the history and the mythology on which so much of our culture is built up, I have given the accounts of this journey, with their constant classical allusions, somewhat fully and with the dignity of a separate episode. The *pièce de resistance* is the long account Patrick designed for insertion in Charles Lister's life; it arrived just too late for use there, and has never been published. Since its centre is naturally Charles's personality, rather than Patrick's, I have filled out the picture with some extracts from the long letters Patrick had time to write during the slow voyage. It occupied the whole of March, and practically all April.

Patrick Shaw-Stewart.

'The cruise of the Hood Battalion in the *Grantully Castle* falls naturally into two parts with an interlude. We sailed from Avonmouth (with the Anson Battalion also on board), on February 28, 1915, arrived in Mudros harbour (Lemnos) on March 11, passed a fortnight of inactivity there, diversified by training ashore, various wild rumours, and one mysterious early morning " feint " journey by the Gallipoli coast, sailed for Egypt about March 24, reached Port Said about 27th, and landed next day. Then followed the interlude—some twelve days in camp in the desert close to Port Said, with forty-eight hours' leave to Cairo in batches of three. The second cruise began about April 11, when the Hood (but not the Anson) re-embarked on the *Grantully Castle* and returned to Mudros, whence, for lack of harbour-room, we were shifted to Scyros; in Scyros harbour we stayed from about 17th to 25th April. On 22nd Rupert Brooke died, and was buried ashore on the evening of the 23rd; on the 24th we sailed for Gallipoli, and on the evening of the 25th took part in the R.N.D.'s demonstration in Xeros Bay, in accordance with the landing scheme.

'In the first stage we suffered from two disadvantages: overcrowding and lack of Charles. The Anson were exceedingly pleasant shipmates, but both they and we cordially agreed that the *Grantully Castle* was not constructed for two battalions and envied the luck (or skill) of the Howe —the third battalion of our Brigade—in developing meningitis just before embarkation and thus securing

Patrick Shaw-Stewart.

a magnificent ship all to themselves. Our men were terribly crowded; the Fleet Reserve men took it as Fleet Reserve men would, while the recruits were for some time too sick to notice it. The officers also suffered slightly in the single drawing-room (constructed to hold a round half-dozen of " intermediate " Union Castle passengers), and now pressed into the service of some seventy of us, including the august Brigade staff, in the mess, where it was not then possible to group ourselves entirely to our fancy, and in the cabins—though here the evil was mitigated by judicious combination, and I had the fortune to share a cabin with Denis Browne, most delightful of companions and most good-natured and unselfish of mankind. There were also comic difficulties in the way of Individual Instruction of Platoons: no one who has not tried it knows what it is like to take a " strong " platoon as a semaphore signalling class in the space afforded by about two yards of casing and the deck corresponding thereto, or how irresistibly interesting in such circumstances —to professor and student alike—are the activities of one's next door neighbours. I, for instance, on these occasions was between Johnny Dodge and Rupert Brooke, and my platoon's development must have sadly suffered from the magnetic influence exercised on me by the gently penetrating Americanisms, and tireless oratorical resources, of the one, and the rich fancies of the other garbed in curt and telling prose. I have said that at that period we lacked Charles; he made, however, a meteoric appearance

Patrick Shaw-Stewart.

on the day we spent at Malta, greatly impressing our naval eyes with his Jodhpore breeches, and, during our stay in Mudros harbour, he was hard by on the dignified *Franconia*, so that dinners could be exchanged, and one day he bicycled with Arthur Asquith and me to Kastro—a notable day, in the course of which Arthur Asquith tried on the inhabitants his Arabic, Charles his Turkish, and I my rudimentary Greek, and I was once more reminded to my delight of Charles's habit, immortalised by Ronald Knox in the phrase " descending obliquely from his bicycle." Finally, when we arrived at Port Said, Charles displayed unmistakable signs of wishing to exchange his position of Divisional Interpreter for a platoon in the Hood. Rupert, Arthur Asquith, and I, left him in the moment of victory installed in that exceedingly sandy camp, and went joyously off for forty-eight hours leave in Cairo, where we luxuriated in almost forgotten comforts and explored with mastery, thanks to Arthur's Arabic, and where Rupert scored his usual success. When we returned to Port Said, " A " Company was full, commanded by Freyberg, with Nelson second, the four platoons being led by Johnny Dodge and myself, Charles and Rupert, in that order. Seldom can two neighbouring platoons of the Army, New or Old, have been more notably led. No sooner were we complete, no sooner had Charles begun to apply his troop-leading lore to his naval bipeds, and to fill the camp with his superb parade voice, than **we were reduced.** The day after

Patrick Shaw-Stewart.

we came back from Cairo I got a touch of the sun, which began as a violent headache and then shifted the scene of its ravages downwards, and retired sick to the Casino Hotel. Two days later I was joined by Rupert, who had the same complaint but worse, with high fever; he was put in my room because the hotel was full, and because I thought I was well, but I relapsed slightly and in the end we shared that room for a week, completely starved (with one or two adventures in eggs and the little sham soles of the Mediterranean, which brought about relapse and repentance), and weak as kittens, disabilities which did not prevent me from enjoying it greatly. This enjoyment was perhaps not diminished by the thought of the wind-swept camp, where one of our stokers remarked that the continual absorption of particles of sand was rapidly forming in his interior a tomb-stone, the removal of which would, he felt, present a problem.

'Charles, among others, visited us in our affliction and diverted us enormously with his adaptation of the Staff publication, *Notes on the Turkish Army*, which became in his hands a string of irreverent *Notes on the R.N.D.* Rupert and he were already friends; previously they had not only known each other by reputation, but met in the flesh at a mixed gathering of the Oxford and Cambridge Fabian Societies.

'Rupert and I were trundled on board the *Grantully Castle* when the battalion pushed off rather hastily about April 11, this time meaning business. Our protestations of fitness were true in my case

Patrick Shaw-Stewart.

but not in Rupert's, although after two or three days in his cabin he began to get up and go about, officially well but really pulled down. On this voyage the Hood had the *Grantully* to themselves, which vastly improved every one's temper and enjoyment. It further enabled a rearrangement of tables in the dining-saloon, and a table was formed consisting of Charles, Rupert, Arthur Asquith, Denis Browne, Cleg Kelly, Johnny Dodge, and myself, under the presidency of one of the ship's officers, who was occasionally, I think, a little surprised at our conversation. I subsequently happened to hear that this table was known to the others as "the Latin Club"; I do not know what piece of pedantry on whose part was responsible for the title. Certainly some noteworthy conversations were held there; it seemed always somehow to happen that we were left there at dinner among the patient stewards, long after everyone else had gone, experimenting on the rather limited repertory of the ship's vintages, and amusing one another none too silently. I wish I could recapture something of the subject-matter: it ranged from the little ways of Byzantine emperors to the correct way of dealing with Turkish prisoners; music, in spite of organised opposition by such Philistines as myself, could not be altogether denied its place; and Johnny Dodge, from time to time, by his radiant devotion to business, forced us to consider such stern matters as iron rations and Column of Blobs. We all read *Duffer's Drift*, we painted

Patrick Shaw-Stewart.

our holsters green to go with our webbing—green as our war experience—we were convinced that the campaign would most unfortunately be ended in a month by the R.N.D. occupying the entire Gallipoli peninsula and setting its foot on the neck of the Turks; we were very wise indeed. But always, whatever the matter in hand, Charles and Rupert delighted each other and the rest of us; they also walked on deck together, and I suspect talked of less hilarious and more permanently significant things. Meanwhile, Cleg Kelly and Denis Browne, encouraged by Charles, stealthily approached the ship's piano and softly, though not always too softly for some of our seniors (I do not speak of myself), who found the space confined, coaxed from it surprising melodies; the subs of " A " Company diced for night watches, and Charles, Rupert, and Johnny Dodge (in fact, all except me), were exceedingly unselfish in this delicate connection; and about April 17 we anchored in the southern bay of Scyros, that smelt to heaven of thyme.

'Here, next day, Charles and I wandered all over the south half of the island in brilliant sunshine and sweet smelling air: we were fed on milk and goat's cheese by a magnificent islander—whom we identified with Eumæus—in his completely Homeric steading, were rowed back to our ship by another sturdy Greek fisherman and his still sturdier wife, and were greeted over the ship's side with slight sarcasm by Rupert, who had taken our watches and suffered endless boredom to enable us to overstay

Patrick Shaw-Stewart.

our scheduled time without dire consequences. Here we floundered about on precipitous perfumed hill-sides packed with spring flowers and sharp stones, in the throes of Battalion and Divisional Field Days more bewildering, unexpected, and exhausting than any we had previously dreed on the Dorsetshire downs, till Rupert, who would not be left behind, felt tired and went to bed early while we still sat and smoked and talked after dinner. Here, one day after, we knew that the germ of pneumonia had attacked him, weak as he was, in the lip, and I was frightened to see him so motionless and fevered just before he was shifted—lowered over the side in a couch from the *Grantully* to a French hospital ship—and here, after one day more, Charles commanded the burial-party and I the firing-party, when we buried him among the olives of Scyros the night before we sailed for the Peninsula.'

. . . . . .

' This is the *Grantully Castle* (Union Castle Line), and a very comfortable boat. I am sharing a cabin with Denis Browne, who is very jolly, and looking forward enormously to the voyage, which will probably last about three weeks. It is great luck for me to see the Greek Islands (so inexpensively too!), which I have always longed to do. I only hope I may be able to nip over and have a look at Troy. I don't think this is going to be at all a dangerous campaign—we shall only have to sit in the Turkish forts after the Fleet has shelled the unfortunate occupants out of them.' [FEBRUARY 28, 1915.]

Patrick Shaw-Stewart.

'It's been a very jolly voyage and would have been perfect if there weren't so many little irritating parades for no particular purpose except to fill up the stokers' time and waste ours. Also there is the constant difficulty of persuading the stokers to be (a) vaccinated; (b) inoculated. There was one party who absolutely refused (b), and as we can't compel, we had just peacefully to picket them, and give them statistics of the army in France, and reminiscences of S. Africa, the only drawback was that I, the Coy. 2nd in Command, the Coy. Commander, the Commandant, and the Commodore all gave widely different statistics, mine being the most temperate and least effective. We've had the most admirable silhouettes of North Africa, which we've been hugging the last two days; to-day we passed a little island called Galita, and now we've left Tunis behind, and are heading straight for Malta. When I say " behind " it is out of consideration for you; really, my command of " aft," " starboard," " companion," and " alley-way " is superb and elicits the admiration of the stokers.' [MARCH, 1915.]

'The most delicious voyage, just enough swell in the Bay and off Tunis to make me proud of my sailorship, and divine weather. I have read *Beauchamp's Career* (never before: I love it), and Oliver's *Alexander Hamilton*, and Gibbons' *The New Map of Europe*, and some of the *Iliad*. The only very tiresome thing is the night watch: I have had two so far, one from midnight to four a.m., and one from

Patrick Shaw-Stewart.

four to eight a.m., and it would be hard to say which was worse. The stokers are terribly in their element, and constantly tell me how much better things are managed on board ship "in the service." I managed at the last moment to hoist Charles into the expedition, but failed to get him into our battalion, as he stuck at the Divisional Staff, owing to their partiality for Lords, and his well-boomed knowledge of Turkish.' [MARCH 8, 1915.]

'I think I last wrote from Malta, where I spent a joyful evening ashore and went to the opera and tried without any success to buy all the things I lost or omitted before starting. It's rather an attractive town (Valetta, that is), with steep and narrow streets, along which native vehicles drive furiously, and the inhabitants talk a completely unintelligible language, and the purest Italian—as represented by Charles and me—is lavished on them in vain.'
[MARCH 17, 1915.]

'As you know, I love my board ship, and this voyage, despite the fact that most of it has been stationary, is pure joy to me. Heaps of books and bridge and cocktails, and not too much campaigning; and it is particularly lucky to have Oc Asquith and Rupert Brooke, and the musician Denis Browne, in the battalion, as they form a sort of nucleus for human intercourse which in the New Army, the Lord knows, one might easily miss entirely.'
[MARCH 26, 1915.]

Patrick Shaw-Stewart.

'I think if, when you get this letter, you would start sending me a *Daily Mail*, and throw in a Saturday *Westminster* to correct my Toryism, it would do me much good. I am full of tobacco, and living in the country which is the birthplace of all cigarettes; but thank you all the same, as they say. Did I say I should like about two Brand's meat lozenges about once a fortnight, slipped into a letter, as it were, and *not* a lot together? That's all I can think of at present. Oh, yes, and a box of matches.'
[MARCH 26, 1915.]

'The other day I had a little leave and, in the course of it, I detached two bronze animals with *cloisonné* backs, of which the horse with the prickly tail is a B.P. for you, and the rabbit which sits upside down you may give a home to for the present.'
[EASTER, 1915.]

'I have endured the tedium fairly well, beguiled, as it has been, by the most agreeable journeyings in the Ægean, and what would have been a most amusing sojourn in Egypt, if I hadn't succumbed to the sun. I got a sun-headache followed by an internal derangement which has compelled me (and Rupert Brooke, who fell a victim soon after) to exchange our canvas for the really quite comfortable —— Hotel, and our bully-beef for arrowroot. To-day it is a sandstorm, and we are thanking our stars for our affliction.'
[EASTER MONDAY, 1915.]

Patrick Shaw-Stewart.

'I am feeling very muzzy this morning because so many people are talking, but before the mail goes out I shall probably remember dozens of wants. We are on a new island this time, not unconnected with the education of Neoptolemus. There is no reason now why I shouldn't say we were at Port Said, as you may probably have divined, and that I went to Cairo for my forty-eight hours leave—it is a perfectly delicious place, and I think I was very lucky to get there for nothing, don't you? It's one of the places I've always wanted to go to. I saw the sphinx and the pyramids (on a camel), and the little temple of Ghizeh and the Australians' camp close by, and the Citadel, and the Mosques of Sultan Hussein and Mohammed Ali (the latter one of the things I like best, but your true Cairene thinks it most out of place and Stamboulesque), and the tombs of the Caliphs by moonlight, on those magnificent Egyptian donkeys which gallop cheerily for miles with a ton weight on their backs, and, of course, the bazaars. Best of all were the creature comforts of Shepheard's Hotel and having one's breakfast in bed there—but I made the mistake of not putting down my net the first night and got soundly bitten. The only thing I regret is that we weren't in Alexandria instead of Port Said—but as I was on my back most of the time it didn't make much difference. As soon as I got on board ship again I felt a different creature, and the last few days I have been careering like a young he-goat over the rockiest island in the Mediterranean. Perhaps a still

Patrick Shaw-Stewart.

stronger test of my vigour is that I've been reading Morley's *Life of Gladstone*.'   [APRIL 25, 1915.]

To Edward Horner.

' As the war goes on I lose none of my old illogical aversion to being dead (though I constantly hum to myself " ac velut anteacto nil tempore sensimus ægri . . ." and then " sic ubi non erimus . . ." and all the other unanswerable Lucretian arguments). I don't now think that I shall run away, but I don't feel at all sure that I shan't do something catastrophically foolish from (a) lack of sense of direction; (b) lack of mechanical knowledge; (c) general lack of bushranging efficiency; or—who knows ? (d) lack of a musical ear (from mistaking the Charge for the Retire).'   [APRIL 15, 1915.]

' Rupert Brooke suddenly sickened and died in thirty-six hours of virulent blood-poisoning. He had never got quite well, like I did, from that illness at Port Said, and so he was in a weak state for resistance. He died the day we left the island, and that same night we took him ashore, and the eight Petty Officers of the Company performed the considerable feat of carrying the coffin a mile inland, in the dark, up-hill, along the most fearfully stony track. I had to command the firing-party, which was anxious work, as I am not strong on ceremonial drill, but all went well.'   [APRIL 25, 1915.]

To R. A. Knox.

' This is a pleasant cruise. How can I describe it uncensoriously ? First to the island of Hephæstus

Patrick Shaw-Stewart.

(or Philoctetes, or Hypsipyle) for a longish stay; then to the Pelusiac mouth to a town famed for its low life, where I escaped a too-sandy camp; then to the island where the fleet-footed Æacid hid *sub lacrimosæ Trojæ funera,* and his son enjoyed the advantages of a classical education; and whence the bones of Theseus were taken home. It is now thirdly bound up with Rupert Brooke, whom we buried there, and over whose grave I commanded the firing-party; an olive grove looking southwards on the Ægean, and what more could a poet ask? He was a very jolly man, and I was sad about it: I shouldn't have thought that any one, in three months, could come to fill so large a space in my life. In return, we have wrested Charles from the Divisional Staff, and his incomparable personality enlivens the battalion. He and I command adjacent platoons: the next was Rupert's πόθεόν γε μὲν ἄρχον.

'Thence we came almost straight to the very edge of the tyranny of Miltiades, in sight of the *notissima fama insula,* in sight of Samothrace, in imaginary sight of windy Ilios itself, and not so very far from Ægospotami; and on this association-saturated spot they propose, I believe, to shove us ashore almost immediately to chase the Turk. The stiffest work has been done already: the landing must have been an amazing performance by Australians and the 29th; but no doubt there's still some walking (shall we say?) for us to do.'

[APRIL 29, 1915].

Patrick Shaw-Stewart.
To His Sister.

' The last two days we've been on the spot, listening to the most prodigious bombardment that ever was. It seems amazing that any Turks can have lived through it, but they have, the devils, and given our first landing-party a poorish time, I'm afraid. But from what we have just heard they have done magnificently. Both the Australians (and N.Z.) and the 29th accomplished a miraculous landing; I'm glad it wasn't us who had to do it, because, though our men will probably be very steady, I doubt if they are quite the raging fiends the Australians seem to be when they're roused—which made that landing possible. I think the heaviest work has been done already, and the remainder will be very exciting, but not anything like so difficult and dangerous.' [APRIL 29, 1915.]

Chapter Seven

Patrick remained on the Peninsula right up to the time of the evacuation, and, indeed, from the point of view of the French contingent, with whom he was serving at the end of the campaign, was one of the very last to leave it; he has sent several sketches of his feelings at that pathetic yet historic moment in the war. The radius of his journeying is now singularly restricted; except for two days at Athens, Imbros is his only change of air, and even on the Peninsula it is almost as if he were fighting in a different theatre of war from his brother Basil, who was at Suvla, only a few miles away. But this geographical restriction brings with it an enhanced value of detail which makes these letters perhaps the most human of the whole collection. The lark that rose out of a pile of Turkish dead, the cake that was commended by General Birdwood, the blue jays and the cranes, and the sea-bathing—these are the incidents we might have missed, and regretted missing, if he had been moving up and down the far-flung battle-line of the Western Front.

Patrick's useful knowledge of French involved his being called upon at times, when the official interpreters were out of action, to act as *liaison* officer with the French. In the end, this appointment was regularised, and he was thus for a time out of the fighting, so far as it was possible for any

Patrick Shaw-Stewart.

one to be out of the fighting in a campaign where every Divisional Staff was in easy range of the enemy's batteries. But this was only after the Hood Battalion had changed its cadre almost entirely, when Denis Browne had been killed, (Charles Lister died of wounds soon after), and others of his friends were away in hospital. The sense that he was still dangerously employed, and that old companions no longer needed him saved him from the *ennui* which he afterwards felt at Salonica.

Ashore.
'We have been ashore now for about ten days. At first sight one might think it was more, but I think that's about it. One's sleep comes at such unofficial hours now, that time becomes a little difficult to reckon. It is a strenuous life, quite a change from the lotus-eating days one spent on board ship—on the whole, I like it more than I expected; one's meals are so delicious and sleep such a luxury; as for a bathe in the sun, which I have brought off twice, it was absolutely divine.'

[MAY 8, 1915.]

Fighting.
'I suppose every one feels much as I do after a week or so of war, it is very exciting, and a thing a man should not have missed; but now I've seen it and been there and done the dashing, I begin to wonder whether this is any place for a civilised man, and to remember about hot baths and

Patrick Shaw-Stewart.

strawberries and my morning *Times*. We have been a good bit in the trenches (I am lying in a reserve one now, just in case the enemy's shrapnel should be wider of the mark than usual), and twice in action. The second day was exciting enough for any one: my next-door neighbour hit four times, and me finding myself to my great surprise in a position so much in front of the army that I had to pretend to be a daisy and crawl away with a few men at dusk. Since then I have been hit at three yards range with an accidental shot plumb on the right heart, where the bullet lodged in my trusty Asprey steel mirror —almost as good an advertisement for that firm as Ock's wound for the Government.'

[MAY 8, 1915.]

' Looking back on the last fortnight (from which we are now resting), I see really nothing much except one day's advance—and *then* I never saw a live Turk that I could swear to. To-day I am much more interested in Nature—the most divine poppies and vetches making the whole place red and blue, and a quite black cypress grove full of French artillerymen down which I took 100 stokers this morning to bathe sumptuously in the actual Dardanelles themselves! And the great and startling beauty of blue jays and cranes, the latter as large and frequent as aeroplanes. (Ibycus did himself proud in birds.[1]) By the way, I bartered

[1] The murderers of Ibycus, according to Greek legend, were betrayed by a flock of cranes.

Patrick Shaw-Stewart.

four pots of jam with the above mentioned French artillery for four loaves of bread (we have nothing but biscuit so far in the British Army), and had a great scene marching triumphantly into our camp with *boules* tucked under each arm. On the strength of this feat I have been made Mess President—an arduous post.

'Another aspect of creation which is of vital interest is the insect department. Besides centipedes and other monsters, this peninsula is marvellously rich in various species of ants, spiders, and beetles, with which, in our troglodytic life, one becomes curiously familiar. I am constantly reminded of the invocation of Achilles in the *Iliad* which mentions the Selloi, a peculiar tribe of dervishes sacred to Zeus, "who couch on the ground and never wash their feet."[1] The former prescription I have complied with rigorously for the last fortnight, and the latter I have broken very seldom. I am slightly surprised, not so much at my health, which I knew I could trust, as at my absence of tiredness. Three nights running (with the fight in between) I had practically no sleep, as one can't trust the Petty Officers to control the men's fire in the first line trenches—and I really felt as fresh as a lark at the end of it. The great advantage is the warmth of the day, which compensates for the very chilly nights—of course one has to dress for both at the same time, which is perplexing. . . . The nearest approach to billets is this backwood

[1] The Selli (Il. xvi. 235).

Patrick Shaw-Stewart.

camp which we are in now, which by comparison is comfortable enough but still means sleeping on the good brown soil—also from time to time it occurs to the enemy to shell one; but far more disturbing are our own guns, which make absolutely the hell of a noise, and the habit which the Senegalese (French niggers) have of letting off their pieces all night long to keep their spirits up. The first night we were next them we thought there must be the hell of an attack coming, and peered anxiously through the night at our wire entanglements, but subsequently we discovered it was just their little way.' [MAY 13, 1915.]

Some Wants.

' Malted milk and gelatines are wonderful to carry in the pocket, but one isn't always on the march, and the amount of more solid and luxurious food one can consume at one meal is surprising—so that some more unpractical non-portable treats like that first lot of shortbread, or any sort of cakey substance, would be most acceptable. Another great idea which has struck me, is that you might get hold of a bottle of *good old* brandy and send it out, a wee flaskful in each parcel. Yet another thing is that chocolate goes in a *flash*, and one can't have enough—another still is that *butter* is a wonderful treat and can be had in very good tins. (I enclose a small cheque to regularise all these very heavy demands, which I want carried out *lavishly*, as there are other hungry mouths besides mine, and one has

Patrick Shaw-Stewart.

to share all round.) On the other hand, cease to bother about shaving sticks, as I have grown a beautiful red beard. On the other hand, socks, bootlaces, and note-paper (plenty of it) always wanted, and pencils and matches. Oh, and I want a *really good* air cushion, that must be tested by *sitting* on it—the fattest shopwalker—for a good stretch, as they nearly all leak if you put them under the hip-bone, and you wake up collapsed on the hard earth.' [MAY 13, 1915.]

To His Nurse.—In Rest.
'A lovely pair of drawers arrived yesterday, which I am now wearing with great pride, having prepared myself for them by bathing in the sea yesterday afternoon, and getting rid of some of the dust and dirt of the trenches. (Dust is better than mud anyhow, and hot than cold.) We had been to the French camp to try and buy wine, and so bathed near there—and the difficulty we had to get out of the range of dead horses in the sea was something painful. There's no doubt, Dear, that that's the worst part of war—the dead bodies of man and beast. There was another heap of dead in front of the trench, and at dawn a lark got up from there and started singing—a queer contrast. Rupert Brooke could have written a poem on that, rather his subject.' [MAY 23, 1915.]

'Three days ago we came up here, and I have sat peacefully in the reserve trenches all the time, as

Patrick Shaw-Stewart.

somebody had made a fuss about the stokers having had too much to do. As a matter of fact, the men have to do all the fatigues when they are in reserve, and hate it accordingly, but for the sub. it is delicious, as he can sleep all night. Also there is a fine prickly heather growing near here, which one can nip out and cut after dark and which makes my dug-out into a feather bed, also I am at the un-whiffy end with no dead Turks near, so I'm very well off.'
[JUNE 1, 1915.]

Rupert Brooke.
'He was a delicious companion, full of good jokes and perfect at other people's. He held the most violent and truculent opinions, and with the gentlest manner you ever saw. I think he had drawn in his horns and abandoned his insolence (as some others of us have tried to do) for the war, in order to live happily with queer hotch-potchy brother officers. He will be a great legend now and have a great fame: it is encouraging to know that his poetry is good enough to stand on its own merits: a soldier-poet's death casting a lustre over fairly but not very good poetry would have been awful, wouldn't it?' [JUNE 2, 1915.]

A Night Advance.
'It's wonderful how people dig in these circumstances (we expected to be attacked, but the Turks were too great mugs)—I myself dug briskly for half an hour, at the end of which my hand was

Patrick Shaw-Stewart.
covered with blisters, so I walked up and down the line instead, asking the men why the hell they didn't dig quicker. We expected the day to reveal the Turks about twice as far off as it actually did, so we all were both surprised and pleased to find where we had quite accidentally got to. My section finished up opposite two heaps of very dead Turks (that element is to my mind the worst in war), and I was moved to head a party of volunteers to bury them at dawn; but they began to fire at us before we had properly finished, so we had to let them continue to remind us of their presence all day.' [JUNE 2, 1915.]

To Lady Desborough.—The Fourth of June.
' You can imagine what I have felt about the two of them ' (Julian Grenfell and Edward Horner, both wounded) ' and thinking of you out there. In ordinary times I could have thought of nothing else, but two days after I was forced to think very hard about my own battalion, who suffered cruelly in a charge on a Turkish trench on the Fourth of June, in which out of fifteen officers left six were killed, including Denis Browne, and five wounded, leaving only me and three others now. I was filled with disgust and rage at the crushing folly of it for a time, but my native stolidity asserted itself—with the result that two *others* out of the four of us left have been sent to Alexandria for a rest, and two of us are carrying on! ' [JUNE 9, 1915.]

Patrick Shaw-Stewart.

To His Sister.
'I cabled to you because I thought you might be alarmed by the Fourth of June casualty lists. That was a cruel day for the 2nd Naval Brigade, because, having taken a Turkish trench we had to abandon it again, our right being exposed and the line enfiladed, and as you will see the losses were very heavy. Denis Browne was killed. . . . I myself was in a position of complete safety with the Brigade H.Q., as at the last moment they fished me out to talk French to the gunner observer (we had French artillery supporting us), and apparently they couldn't find any one else whose French was sufficiently marketable. Undoubtedly a good job for me, and shows the advantages of a sound commercial education. It may easily happen again on a similar occasion, and should be meditated on as a prophylactic against nerves on my account. I am becoming known on the Peninsula as the "*liaison* officer." For the moment, till some of the wounded seniors roll up again, I am in command of a company. I have positively two sub's at my disposal, and you should see me ordering them about. But I am really very kind and thoughtful.'

[JUNE 13, 1915.]

A New Enemy.
'Are there such things as powders which make up into lime-juice and other such drinks? And could you send a sparklet? Petroleum pomade arrived safely but rather pervasively. I want you

Patrick Shaw-Stewart.

to think of every conceivable means of attack and defence against FLIES, which are getting the very devil. The following occur to me : (1) Fly-papers (*numbers*); (2) Fly-whisks; (3) Some sulphuric apparatus for smoking them out—must work easily; (4) Khaki (brown and green) motor-veils —two or three, so as I can give to the deserving.'
[JUNE 13, 1915.]

To Lady Desborough.—*Julian Grenfell.*
'. . . When I was going to Dunkirk in a great hurry in September, and longing for expert advice, I heard he was in London and I made him come round to Little Grosvenor Street and give me tips. Edward turned up at the same moment, and (in spite of my abundant terror of war) we had a hilarious morning. They each put on my Sam Browne, which was rather a peculiar one, in a different way, and Edward (who was wrong) prevailed. Julian was rollicking, just like earliest Balliol, and looking rather funny and very adorable. He gave me his sword because I couldn't get one in time, and he said he was going to use a trooper's " because he could do more killing with it." I have written down this bare chronicle because it has been running in my head. You might mind very much having all those golden years—as most of them were—recalled to you, but I am almost sure you won't. I think I am most tremendously lucky to have had Julian in my life as long and as closely as I did. It is not many who have such a glowing fire to warm their

Patrick Shaw-Stewart.

hands at. We quarrelled some times, but always slightly. Julian was often immeasurably shocked with me, chiefly (directly or indirectly) at my habit of trying, to the best of my power, to arrange things ahead in my life, to tabulate, and to reduce to as little as possible the pressure of blind circumstance, which, God knows, must anyhow be big enough. He was, of course, always for *letting things happen to him* (perhaps he scarcely realised how his personality made at least some things happen to him which others would have had to seek out with labour) and making happy improvisations. It spoiled a thing for him, even a house-party, if it was obviously well arranged beforehand. I think he dealt hardly with the powers of his own mind. He cramped them to make room for action. Also, he was put off by the disappointments due to his illness. I wish he had been perfectly well all those years at Oxford. He had unexampled and endless freshness of viewpoint, than which nothing is more valuable. His last poem is an amazing message to get from him, like others out here, with the news of his death.'

[JUNE 22, 1915.]

The Historical Setting.—To R. A. Knox.
 ' You never enclosed that copy of verses after all. Do so now, and further, please do something for me which will keep you usefully employed for no mean time. Trace me a good-sized map of this part of the world (including Chersonese up to Kardia—Bulair, the Troad, Tenedos, Lemnos, Imbros),

Patrick Shaw-Stewart.
and fill in all the classical topography you can muster, particularly on the Chersonese itself, where at least the following should be marked :—Elæus, Madytus (? Maidos), Sestos, Pactya, Kardia, Ægospotami—these mostly from Herodotus, whom I have with me; but besides that I want the topography from the Hellenica and other relevant works, *and a historical monograph to elucidate it,* as I know nothing outside the Herodotean facts. The monograph should include Alexandrian and Roman times—I am sure that either Sulla or Lucullus or Pompey must have been round here—and should have an appendix on Byzantine and Venetian periods—in fact, it might be brought up to date. Do do this abundantly, it would be enormous fun for me. (The historical sketch need only be minute on the Chersonese—just a note or two on the Troad and the three islands.) At present I feel a hideous uncertainty about even simple things like Ægospotami—should it or should it not be identified with Morto Bay?

' To-night I am not sorry to be ordered to go for a brief rest to the island whither Miltiades escaped the Phenicians (but he lost his son).'

[JUNE 19, 1915.]

To His Sister.—Imbros.
' Imbros was delicious. It is a prettier island than Lemnos, and with nicer villages, Panagia and Kastro. And the simple joy of being out of shell-fire after two months of it was considerable. To

Patrick Shaw-Stewart.

live in a tent (they are too conspicuous to be allowed here) instead of a dug-out was also jolly, and as I was temporarily commanding a company I had one to myself. I went over as often as I could from our camp at Kephalos on the east to Panagia over the central ridge and Kastro on the west, where there was delicious coffee and beer and eggs and mullets and marvellous mulberries that dropped into your mouth and covered you all over with blood-red stains that turned blue-black, and you could forget for a day that you were a damned soldier, and talk as best as you could to the amiable Greeks. One of them said to me, " Turkoi skotountai polu ? " which I boldly guessed to mean " Are the Turks being much whacked ? " and I said, " Yes, rather," and, in case there should be any doubt, added that we had killed 50,000 and taken 5000 prisoners—so it's not my fault if Imbros doesn't come in, with or without Tino. But most of the time we had to parade and drill—you see, you can never parade here or speak to more than six men at a time, for fear of shells, which is bad for their souls—and that was tiring. I'm now second in command of " D " Company (mostly stokers, though not my old ones), having been relieved in command by Ock, who is three days senior to me! Fortunately I have not violent military ambitions and am delighted to have him back, also Charles; they both came the same day.' [JUNE 30, 1915.]

' As the fatigues seemed fixed for ten days ahead,

Patrick Shaw-Stewart.

and as I had just escaped liability to them by being gloriously promoted to Lieut. R.N.V.R. (= Captain in army—either address may be employed—English papers please copy), I thought the moment had come to have my teeth doctored. So, dexterously acquiring merit by waiving my claim to Alexandria, I took a week's leave on Imbros, and here I am, living in a Greek village and talking the language of Demosthenes to the inhabitants (who are really quite clever at taking my meaning). It is very pleasant to live outside a dug-out for a few days, and only to hear the guns modified by fifteen miles of water.'

[JULY 10, 1915.]

To Edward Horner.

'That flower of sentimentality which buds rather unreadily in me expands childishly on classical soil. It is really delightful to me (I expect it would be to you) to bathe every day, when not in the trenches or standing by, in the Hellespont, looking straight over to Troy, to see the sun set over Samothrace, to be fighting for the command of Ægospotami, and to restate Miltiades' problem of the lines of Bulair. Though that damned old Achi-baba (or " Archibald " as we waggishly call it) still frowns at us with an impregnable frown, I am at present disposed to be very optimistic, partly, perhaps, because Charles and Oc have just come back and human relationships thus restarted. Do you remember just before I went to Dunkirk, when you and Julian advised me all one morning how to put on a Sam Browne,

Patrick Shaw-Stewart.

and what to pack in 35 lb. ? We were young, very merry, and not war-wise (*how* well I could pack some young lad's 35 lb. for him now, and how cynically I should explain that he could make it up to 70 lb. with well-timed parcels!). That was the last time I saw Julian, and the only time for nearly two years. I have lost people who left a fresher gap, such as Rupert, or a more continuous one such as John, but never one who was once such a great friend, or who was tied up in my mind with such a solid and distinct block of Balliol life—indeed, short of you and Charles, it would be impossible.'
[JULY 1, 1915.]

' Till two days ago we had done practically nothing since June 4, and about ten days ago we were told to do a solid fortnight of " beach fatigues," and I thought the moment had come to have one or two teeth put right on Imbros. I got a week's leave, and installed myself, not in the rest camp (which is hot and dull and military), but over in the hills in a Greek village, Panagia, where it is cool and delicious and the people amusing and very understanding of ancient Greek. There I spent three days, mostly trudging over to the camp for teeth, and was looking forward to four more of pure fun, when I was suddenly recalled, as we were going up to the trenches.'
[JULY 17, 1915.]

Sir Ian Hamilton's Despatch.
' You can trace the time when we were kicked up

Patrick Shaw-Stewart.

in the middle of the night of the first-second, and took part in the abortive advance of the second a.m. (except a detachment including me which had been sent out to guard the General from snipers the night before, and was late for the battle!), and then when we relieved the French on the afternoon of the fourth (in broad daylight in the open—those were good old days, and I suppose we were 2000 yards from the Turks, instead of fifty, which is the rule nowadays). I am afraid the Hood will never be mentioned much because we never did anything on our own—always together with Howe. The ones who will go down to posterity are the Anson, who were in the landing by themselves, and went over to support the French (see despatch, " one battalion R.N.D.") by themselves, and didn't join us again till May 6. In general, I am bound to say they've had the hardest time—particularly in having *all* their senior people knocked out by June 4, and being since taken over by Marines, and all their individuality squashed out, whereas Hood had always a few old salts like me left to preserve the proper naval tradition and refuse to be bullied. . . .

'The junior *liaison* officer has been badly wounded and the " temporary " is likely to be longish, if they keep me, at present I am on appro.

'Of course there are obvious reasons against leaving one's regiment, especially when it contains jolly people like Charles (who is back again after being particularly gallantly wounded for the second time), and Oc, but on the whole I am quite prepared

Patrick Shaw-Stewart.

to be passive in the matter, and do what the Corps tells me. So for the moment here I am in inglorious safety on the gilded Staff ("acting G.S.O. III.", which *ought* to be paid at the rate of £400 a year), and speaking French for dear life.'
[AUGUST 3, 1915.]

'The fact is there is little news here, we are all waiting with ill-concealed impatience for Basil to make history. In the interest of him and his lot we and the French lost heavily five days ago, but the R.N.D. took no part. In fact, I have so far not only missed no fighting since I left the battalion, but no trenches, as they have all been in corps reserve since 25th July. Some day I will tell you more about this last week, or B. will—I saw those two battles last week painfully well from an observation post with a French Staff officer. I enclose a letter from B. We correspond quaintly across the far-flung line of the Force, which takes about ten days.'
[AUGUST 12, 1915.]

Liaison Officer with the French.
'I am of an accommodating nature, and am delighted to have "a pot of ale and safety." The pot of ale is certainly plentiful—though—as I have excellent opportunities for seeing—the way our Army Headquarters do themselves is a scandal compared to the French. We spend pounds on our mess here and have tons of servants, and yet we never seem to have anything fit to eat, and you always see

Patrick Shaw-Stewart.

the rations thinly disguised under everything that appears. While the French, with far less fuss, make their mess exactly like a Paris restaurant.'

[AUGUST 17, 1915.]

Winter Prospects.—To R. A. Knox.

'Thank you for *three* masterly instalments of the history of the Dardanelles, accompanied by two illuminating maps. Thus equipped, and fortified by Walter Leaf's *Troy*, which I have amassed, I can answer almost any questions, and am constantly astonishing the natives by little voluntary excursus on the deeper significance of the site of their dugout. Several captains of antiquity seem to have grasped the idea of the combined operations, but few can have taken so long over it as us. I am now fully prepared for a (fairly) peaceful old age on the Peninsula, which I would contemplate cheerfully were there greater facilities for leaving it now and then. As it is, the farthest move that can be anticipated is an occasional night on Imbros, which eventually tends to lose its freshness. All that might not be so bad, but when you carefully note the date on this letter, the *month* cannot fail to strike your eye and to induce reflections on Equinoctial Gales and (in general) the Winter Campaign. I wish Sir Ian Julius Cæsar Hamilton would lead back his legions into winter quarters (say) in Alexandria, but I don't suppose he will, and we shall eventually settle by grim experience the question that to-day is anxiously debated in 1000 Chersonesiote messes:

Patrick Shaw-Stewart.

What is the climate of Gallipoli in winter ? My own theory is that it doesn't get really bad till December, and that something will turn up towards the end of November, but I admit that that view expects at least its full share from Heaven.'
["1st september, 1915—Partridge Shooting begins."]

A Visit.
' I have one thing which is not black misery to say a word about. I managed by great ingenuity to get over to S—— to-day (Father's birthday), and saw Basil for an hour or two; in fact, had luncheon with him, and a very good one too, and inspected (from a safe distance) their front under his auspices. He hasn't got a bed, poor lamb, nor a proper fly-net; I will send him your last one.'
[september 9, 1915.]

Charles Lister.—To R. A. Knox.
' I love always to hear from you about people I don't get news of, but I am almost incapable of writing about Billy, Douglas, Charles. I have had to do so much of it. Balliol of our time has had, I do think, a high proportion of killed; my best friends never seem to get comfortably wounded, even Edward was touch and go. I think you and I are the only ones who thoroughly realise the length and breadth of what we lose in Charles. I think from different points of view we have perhaps understood him as well as any one else, and certainly

Patrick Shaw-Stewart.

prized him as highly; and we alone have all College and all Balliol in retrospect of him. He was quite extraordinarily good out here, and supplied an example of how not to grouse, and not to appear unduly to mind being killed, not unneeded by some of the newer drafts of officers. The men, both stokers and recruits, adored him—they always called him "Lord Lister," which conjured up delicious visions of the aged man of science as a company officer. He had really what the despatches call devotion to duty; he was all the time resisting an intrigue by the Intelligence people (fomented by me) to get him moved there, which was on the point of coming off. He was constantly doing the most reckless things, walking between the lines with his arms waving under a hot fire from *both* sides; but his last wound, like his others, was from a shell in a trench, and no blame could attach. I think nothing worse can happen. God and the King have both lost a protagonist, and people like you and me the most divine of men.'

[SEPTEMBER 16, 1915.]

A Voyage from Imbros.

'It was as much as our stout trawler could do to get us here. I *just* wasn't sick—there was a poor Turkish prisoner on board who rendered up all he had all the time over the stern, a little wisp of a man, while a stern British sergeant-major clutched him firmly by the seat of the trousers.'

[SEPTEMBER 23, 1915.]

Patrick Shaw-Stewart.

International Complications.
 'I have got a new coadjutor, who will be where I was. To-day I am to introduce him to the French authorities, an agreeable task I am sure, as they like their occasional Lord even better than we do. "Oui, il est fils de Earl, puis par consequent il est Viscount, ce que nous appelons titre de courtoisie, mais il n'est pas pair," I hear myself in anticipation saying a hundred times.' [OCTOBER 6, 1915.]

The Cake.—To His Nurse.
 ' Own Dear, you are a perfect sweet to have sent those lovely cakes, the one that was like a Scotch bun was a *great* success with the French Staff, who had never tasted anything like it.

 ' I think I am going to end my days on this old Peninsula, not necessarily prematurely, but just because I don't see how I am to get off. However, I have very little to complain of. The senior *liaison* officer has gone away for the time being, and I am the Great Panjandrum myself, and have seven signallers and a Viscount under me! I live in a beautiful little wooden house which has a real tin roof with earth on the top. The weather is still delicious, though it's beginning to cool, and they say it needn't rain till Christmas. Did you ever tell me what a good book *Redgauntlet* is? I read it the other day and *loved* it on the strength of it. I've sent for *Guy Mannering* and *The Heart of Midlothian*, and am going to become a Sir Walterite in my old

Patrick Shaw-Stewart.

age. The one advantage of war is that one has time to read.' [OCTOBER 14, 1915.]

The Elements of a Grouse.—To Edward Horner.
' I suppose the elements of a grouse are to be found in the situation of those of us who have been here—like me—from the beginning: six months in the field and eight months from England, and every prospect of a winter to go on with. Except for two days in Cairo at the end of March, I have not seen a civilised town or a woman or child (bar semi-human Greek villagers) since February. Indeed, I have scarcely seen a *civilian*, and was moved to some emotion by the sight of a French journalist in a straw hat and tweed suit who once ventured on to this place. In the same period in France I suppose I should have had about four leaves. On the other hand, I should very likely be dead, and that is always important, though it is queer enough when you come to think of it that I'm not dead here. On the whole, I'm not sorry to be here; as a retrospect it will be just not so widely-spread (especially the first two or three months) as to be intolerable, which France will be. Nor am I very sorry not to have gone to Salonica, which I was bitten by at first; it will be colder there than here, and the prospect of being between 500,000 Bulgars and at least an equal quantity of Germanics is almost too adventurous for me. But one would at least have got a bath at Salonica on the way, and for that I have a great accumulated longing. [OCTOBER 24, 1915.]

Patrick Shaw-Stewart.

To His Nurse.

'I never told you properly the noble history of your last cake, one of the glorified currant loaf kind with a crust (which keeps them fresh as new-mown hay). General Birdwood was doing temporary Commander-in-Chief in between Sir Ian and Sir Charles Monro, and invited himself to tea with the French General. The latter was in despair at not having anything sufficiently " serious " to offer an English General for tea—knowing that we tend to make a meal of it—and I stepped into the breach with the offer of my " plum cake " (an adopted French word pronounced " ploom kak ") which had then just arrived. It made a noble show in the middle of the table and had the greatest success.

' " Is this from France ? " asked General Birdwood, between two mouthfuls. " No, it is the gift of Capitaine Stuart," said General Brulard. " From Scotland, sir," said I, amid loud cheers. So the cake had really a worthy fate. I am awfully distressed about the jam you talked of. I am afraid that the beach robbers (who are simply unspeakable) must have got at it. I enclose a snapshot of me by a Frenchman, always, as you observe, the cheerful British Army, though not, perhaps, over handsome.

' It's very jolly living with the French, they are so nice, and cheerful, and their food is so good, and their arrangements like clockwork; but oh, how I should like a hot bath, and a stiff shirt, and a dinner at the Ritz, with lots of beautifully dressed young women, smelling of something different from

Patrick Shaw-Stewart.

incinerators and a very dirty sea-shore! Do write.' [ALL SOULS' DAY, 1915.]

Preparations for Winter.—To Raymond Asquith.
'I am bound to admit that the autumn, after a spasm of wind and a shower or two, has settled down to as divine a season as you could well choose (if any one in their senses ever did choose such a thing) for living in the open. We are preparing for the winter after our kind: the British have imported about a dozen footballs, and the French about 3000 bullet-and-rain-proof huts. By the grace of God my own lot is cast with the latter, and I am living like a fair imitation of a gentleman in a little wooden cubicle with a tin roof, where the fleas are dying out as the weather cools, and the rats and mice have not yet assumed really serious proportions. My functions, too, are of the most gentlemanly: I seldom speak to any one under the rank of a colonel, and do not disguise my preference for Major-Generals. A pleasant life, if smacking slightly of eternity, and an unparalleled opportunity for becoming Better Read.' [ALL SOULS' DAY, 1915.]

Settling Down.
'Nothing now, I think, can prevent us staying the winter here, but till January (when there are four months of bad weather) there are many worse places, and then I shouldn't be altogether surprised if I saw you in the spring.'
[NOVEMBER 2, 1915.]

Patrick Shaw-Stewart.

Mixed Reading.—To Lady Desborough.

'I have read *Lord Ormont* and *Redgauntlet* and *Lavengro* and Finlay's *Greece under the Romans,* and *Mademoiselle de Maupin,* and Hewlett's *Open Country,* and some Herodotus, and some Lucretius, and re-read *The Egoist*; and I am reading Bosanquet's *Theory of the State,* and Macaulay's *History,* and *Love and Mr Lewisham*; also I have read some Gibbon, and *Guy and Pauline.* I sustained my opinion of *The Egoist* (which is an exalted one) very completely in re-reading. I have now lent it to a Frenchman who thinks he knows English well, with malicious joy.' [NOVEMBER 2, 1915.]

Partly because literary criticism is so rare in Patrick's letters, I cannot forbear to insert here an extract belonging to a different period, but qualifying his expression of opinion on two of his favourite authors just mentioned—Lucretius and George Meredith. It is concerned *ex professo* with some comments on *The Shropshire Lad* :—

'Such a mistake to put too much hard thinking into one's poetry; it's the mistake Browning and Meredith made: and they both might have done so well, and indeed did, in spite of the gigantic *tour de force* they both undertook. Some day I will show you Lucretius's poem *On the Nature of Things,* to prove what a glorious poet can fall to if he mistakes

Patrick Shaw-Stewart.

the province of poetry. So much on the high level: but *prudentially* I implore you not to go about calling Housman " pretty "—all the great men wear him next their heart, I assure you. All the great men—but not the women, I allow: I only know two who love him. God protect me from generalisations on your sex! but I am tempted to believe that they all like their poetry to Tell them Something—dear Lord, what a misconception.'   [MARCH, 1911.]

. . . .

A Visit to Athens.—*To R. A. Knox.*

' I send you a picture of a church because you are a clergyman. It is a very remarkable church of *circa* 850, and made entirely of ancient chunks, as you may observe. It shows how important it is to know one's Finlay.'   [NOVEMBER 23, 1915.]

To His Sister.

' You can imagine it was a combination of sensations to be in Athens, all the funny old things that I spent my industrious youth in reading up, and on top of that the first glimpse of civilisation since Cairo, *and* the uncertainty as to what the modern Greeks were going to do. Needless to say, I didn't talk politics with them, being only too anxious to look an innocent Swiss civilian, but I'm afraid Tino is popular, and now that they are mobilised only he and his pro-German General Staff really matter.'
[NOVEMBER 25, 1915.]

Patrick Shaw-Stewart.

To Dr Alington:
' A simple calculation reveals the fact that I have now been the better part of ten months from England, and getting on for eight ashore. (That will be truer when it reaches you; I always like to do myself full justice.) It's a much longer period than I have ever stayed in one place before with so few comings and goings, and it certainly is a quaint locality to choose to make one's record of. Broadly speaking, I have disliked it all intensely, but not nearly so much as I disliked the more preparatory stages of the warrior's career on Salisbury Plain last winter. (Probably the only period of the war I have really tolerated was when I was at the Crystal Palace and could dine in London every night.) But on the whole I'm glad I came here and not to France; one will bore one's grandchildren slightly less with one's doddering anecdotes of the Chersonese, because they will be slightly less widespread. (Not but what one will bore them a good deal.) And it is something to have the sun so obliging as to rise beyond Ida and set over Samothrace. And one bit of real genuine fun I have got out of it—forty-eight hours in Athens, for which I machinated for months, and which I brought off three weeks ago. Looking back on it, I find myself tending to dwell perhaps as much on the modern beauties of Athens as on the ancient. Probably the former, to the well-trained eye, are miserable enough, but to the Peninsular veteran they were positively dazzling. The thing that I remember perhaps most distinctly was the

Patrick Shaw-Stewart.

real bath in the hotel; after that, the temple of Nike Apteros, hotly pursued by the Averoff restaurant. Eleusis was disappointing I thought, probably because I wasn't well up in it.'

[NOVEMBER 30, 1915.]

To Lady Desborough.

'We got there on the Saturday morning, and had a gloriously fine afternoon on the Acropolis and in the Acropolis Museum. I was overjoyed with it, having always expected Athens would be disappointing. Then the modern side of it appealed greatly to the Peninsular veteran, and I may as well confess that I spent most of the night in an Athenian night club. (They have an opposite rule to London; you *mayn't* leave before 3 a.m.) In the morning we went to the Museum, full of amazing things, and in the afternoon to Eleusis, where we met seven Germans, *with a dachshund*—a strange sight and sensation, one felt vaguely as if one ought to entrench. During the storm I passed twenty-four hours on a trawler between here and Imbros, unable to land: I never knew before what it was to be Ick.'

[NOVEMBER 30, 1915.]

His New Rank.

'They are going to make me a G.S.O.3. (General Staff Officer 3rd grade) for this job, I believe. It takes about six months to get these things through, but I hope they will antedate when they do. It is worth seeing to that, as it is £400 a year; quite an

Patrick Shaw-Stewart.

advance on the pay of a Lieut. R.N.V.R., even with Field Allowance.

'I've just got Mr Balfour's *Theism and Humanism*, and Wells' *Research Magnificent*. Both most interesting, especially the latter. (Read it.)'

[DECEMBER 7, 1915.]

Evacuation of the Peninsula.
'To-night, I can now say without indiscretion, is the historic night, not altogether glorious, but so far very adroit, of our disappearance from the Peninsula. It's pretty sad when you think of what it has cost us, but since they got German ammunition through, the shelling has been very tiresome, and I am quite persuaded that it's the only thing to do. Only the French guns remain (of the French), and the French C.O. and I have been walking up and down looking unconcerned and smelling the breeze (in case it should develop), and burning anything we think the Turks would enjoy or be able to use. I have burnt some queer things, including a bowler hat.

'Well, I have certainly seen the campaign of the Dardanelles—the beginning, the end, and all the middle. I am lucky to be walking off it, but I mustn't speak too soon, as they are shelling the beach from the region of Troy, and I have got to get on to the *River Clyde* somehow in an hour or two. Meanwhile, I am hanging on to the telephone, which my signallers are itching to dismantle.'

[JANUARY 8, 1916.]

Patrick Shaw-Stewart.

' All day we have been looking at the weather in terror in case the wind should rise, but, thank the Lord, it is still only a gentle breeze. It takes one back to that other night, in April, when we waited on the ship and listened to the terrific bombardment at the landing—now it is just the opposite. I am waiting on shore and it is as quiet as the grave, except when the batteries from Asia send us an occasional shot. If they had any idea of what we are up to they would simply make hay of the beaches, and it's rather satisfactory to feel we are cheating them, and they will wake up in the morning and find us gone.

' But, on the whole, it's nothing to be proud of for the British Army or the French either—nine months here, and pretty heavy losses, and now nothing for it but to clear out.

' I wonder what next?'

[JANUARY 8, 1916.]

' I and the French artillery commander (the only representative of his race now remaining), are passing the afternoon walking up and down with a great appearance of calm, looking at our watches, snuffing the air for the least suspicion of wind that might get up and be a nuisance, and from time to time lighting a new little bonfire and destroying a few more maps or papers (I have burnt a nice suit of khaki drill, a bowler hat, and about twenty books, resolved not to leave the Turks even any intellectual

Patrick Shaw-Stewart.

pabulum). I really feel almost sorry to leave Seddul Bahr after my prodigious stay in it.'
[JANUARY 8, 1916.]

'The French general has put me down for the Legion of Honour, which is very sweet of him, and great fun. I am sorry to part with the French; it has been a very pleasant job as jobs go here, and I have not felt so hopelessly a square peg in a round hole as I have usually felt since the war began.'
[JANUARY 8, 1916.]

The following poem was found written in Patrick's handwriting on a blank page in his copy of *The Shropshire Lad*. It seems clear, from the circumstance that there were corrections in the original, that he wrote it himself, although he does not allude to it anywhere :—

> I saw a man this morning
>   Who did not wish to die:
> I ask, and cannot answer,
>   If otherwise wish I.
>
> Fair broke the day this morning
>   Against the Dardanelles;
> The breeze blew soft, the morn's cheeks
>   Were cold as cold sea-shells.

Patrick Shaw-Stewart.

But other shells are waiting
  Across the Ægean sea,
Shrapnel and high explosive,
  Shells and hells for me.

O hell of ships and cities,
  Hell of men like me,
Fatal second Helen,
  Why must I follow thee?

Achilles came to Troyland
  And I to Chersonese:
He turned from wrath to battle,
  And I from three days' peace.

Was it so hard, Achilles,
  So very hard to die?
Thou knowest and I know not—
  So much the happier I.

I will go back this morning
  From Imbros over the sea;
Stand in the trench, Achilles,
  Flame-capped, and shout for me.

Chapter Eight

THE remaining two years of Patrick's life divide themselves up easily; 1916 was spent in the East again, 1917 (apart from leave) in France. He came home after the failure of our hopes in the Dardanelles, and some of his friends hoped that, since the strain of Gallipoli had made some impression even on his extraordinary constitution, he would be given full time to rest before his services were again called upon. But in the middle of March he found himself at a moment's notice Eastward bound again, ' I think and hope ' (he writes to Dr Alington on March 15), ' to Salonica, to join the French.' The forces at Salonica seemed the legitimate heirs of those who had fought on Gallipoli; everybody prophesied that, one way or another, they had stirring times ahead of them—and indeed, in the event, it was the Bulgars who first asked for an armistice. Patrick's hopes were realised, but he had hardly installed himself at Salonica when he began to repine at the absence of activity and of danger; he hated to think of the Hood Battalion earning fresh laurels in France while he took his tram through Salonica in safety. He made more than one unofficial attempt to get transferred, and finally (as will be seen), applied officially for release; but, by that time in the war, young and brilliant brains were beginning to be estimated at something

Patrick Shaw-Stewart.

of their true value, and the unexpected result of his endeavours was simply to transfer him from Intelligence to Operations, and leave him, as he complained, to stick pins into maps. It was only at the end of the year, when he got leave home, that his personal representations succeeded in winning for him the dangers he coveted.

There were intervals, however, in this period of what he regarded as uselessness; the most noticeable was the French advance in August, 1916, in the course of which Patrick, who had already been decorated with the Legion of Honour in Gallipoli, was cited in Divisional Orders for the Croix de Guerre. His geographical movements during this year are traced for us by a letter he sent on the tenth of November—the letter was not going by post to England, so that he felt justified in taking the opportunity of giving the key to his changes of scene. During April and May he was in the Kukus (Kilkish) district. During May and June, at Likovan and on the Struma in late June, Kukus again. In July, with the other French near Snevce, and over the mountains near Dora Tepa to Lake Butkova and the junction of the Butkova and Struma, and the Krusha Balkan to the South. August, September, and October, back with the old lot of French on the Doiran front, at Kilindir, Doldzeli, Hersova, and in the hills south-east of Lake Doiran.

Patrick Shaw-Stewart.

En Route for Salonica.
  'Don't bother about me. I have got a beautiful Gieve (the gift of ——), and wear it as near my heart as convenient. Also we are sailing from Devonport, and avoiding the Channel, which is a dead safe thing to do. Subs don't flourish in Biscay Bay, the Mediterranean is practically all right now they say. As for out there, as you know, *liaison* officers don't do much fighting, and there isn't any at all anyhow at S——, or likely to be in a great hurry. I told you, didn't I, that they've made me a soldier, a Captain, with an option of returning to the R.N.D. if I want to later? I am entirely covered with red tabs, and am looked on with holy awe by all the junior subs on board.' [MARCH 15, 1916.]

To R. A. Knox.
  'I do hope you're getting on well—write and let me know. I think (unofficially) I'm going to Salonica, so the moment you're well, I shall want an ancient map of Southern Macedonia and the Chalcidice and a work on Mount Athos and a brochure of Macedonian history from the earliest times! Not really all that, but, anyhow, get well quickly.' [MARCH 15, 1916.]

To His Sister.
  'I have read quite a lot: *Homer and History* by Walter Leaf, *The Geographical Aspect of Balkan Problems* by some female don (very dry), Macaulay's

Patrick Shaw-Stewart.

History (progress made), finished Flaubert's *Education Sentimentale* (a triumph), Thais again, *La-bas* by Huysmans (mostly about devil-worship), A. E. W. Mason's *Mystery of the Villa Rose* in Spanish, Edgar Vincent's *Modern Greek*, Henry James's *Washington Square*, some Lucretius, and a lot of Eddie's *new* Georgian Poets, which I think are better than the old. We had a submarine scare, but the sea looked so warm and inviting, and my Gieve waistcoat so saucy when inflated, that I was quite disappointed it didn't develop.' [MARCH 24, 1916.]

Impressions of the New Front.
 ' Here (a) there is no war going on; (b) if there was I shouldn't be near it; (c) it is safer than England, because the Germans have now promised the Greek Government there shall be no more air-raids on Salonica. Really it is rather absurd. I went yesterday (by motor and horse) to the so-called front, which looked more like a garden-city than anywhere else, to eyes accustomed to the Chersonese. Rows of happy Tommies were putting the last touches to trenches already finished off almost beyond human perfection. I am truly sorry for the Bulgar who may try to take them one day. But, of course, the real front is on the frontier with the cavalry, or at least that's as near to a front as we can produce here. The French and British Headquarters are at opposite ends of the town and the *liaison* conveys himself from one to the other (when he can't pinch the Staff motor) by the ordinary tram

Patrick Shaw-Stewart.

of commerce, instead of the picturesque ride over shell-swept beaches at Helles.'   [APRIL 7, 1916.]

'And yet, so ungrateful is human nature that it only makes me feel as I'm not fighting I might just as well be in real town—Cairo, for instance, or even London. Certainly the weather here is delicious, the time of year just right, all the little necessities of life, like the wash, and hot water, and drinks, amply supplied, and an opportunity for learning Greek. Unfortunately, just as I had collected a teacher with some care, I find I am sent up country for an indefinite time. It will be just the same sort of garrison life as here, but slightly more to do (with luck), and lots of riding and ground game they say, if not quite so much to eat and drink. If only I had some works of reference here, I should write such a good book. As it is, the only thing to write is a novel—and, curiously, I don't feel inspired, whereas three years ago, when I was very busy at Barings, I was bursting with them. To-day I secured a car, and tried to go to Pella (Alexander's birthplace) but of course the beastly thing had *three* punctures on the way, and all I could do was to look at it through my glasses from the top of a mound.'

[APRIL 17, 1916.]

To Lady Desborough.
'Nothing can conceal from me the fact that I am superfluous here: they have enough *liaison* already, and even when (or if) this front becomes active, I

Patrick Shaw-Stewart.

shall not be what Lord Kitchener (I think) calls "pulling my weight." Therefore (don't tell any one), I am seriously considering applying to "return to duty," either in the R.N.D., or (if they are quite effete) in the Army.' [APRIL 18, 1916.]

The Country.
'A new feature is supplied by several terrifying brands of Macedonian serpent, most of them, I believe, innocuous, but that doesn't prevent me exploring my flea-bag with an electric torch before slipping into it, or shaking my boots vigorously of a morning.

'The country has chased my microbes, and made me quite tired and happy. Even our cook can be circumvented by the aid of eggs and *yourt* (the famous Metchnikoff sour milk, which becomes quickly a habit and then a passion). [IRIKLI, APRIL 24, 1916.]

To Lady Desborough.
'I must correct (provisionally) the impression of gloom and discontent I gave you in my last letter. Almost immediately after writing it, I left Salonica, and the country has (as they say) cleared the cobwebs out of my brain. The old perpetual *fête-champetre*, less the dug-out and the enemy; all the other familiar facts, plus terrifying Macedonian snakes of gigantic proportions, and a spaciousness really quite amazing to a Gallipoli veteran, for whom a waddle of 200 yards was the last word in military locomotion. Now it is interminable rides in every

Patrick Shaw-Stewart.

direction in (mostly) lovely spring weather, with a thought too much sun, and a great number of storks, magpies, and tortoises; really rather jolly, as I have a fairly sound, though horribly lazy, piebald horse.'
[APRIL 26, 1916.]

To Raymond Asquith.
' On reaching Salonica I found (as I had expected) that no one had ever heard of me. Egypt, on being rather testily appealed to, confirmed but failed to particularise, so that my subsequent career has been a trifle hazy. The first part was a fortnight in Salonica, where I was clearly superfluous. The second part has been rural, at different minor H.Q., and has consisted largely in coping with torrential spring rains in an imperfect bivouac. I have rather lost the habit of discomfort, and was at first inclined to take things hardly, but the spirit of my race has reasserted itself. I am trying to learn Greek, but the worst is (see any recent Balkan literature) that unless you are also equipped with Serb, Bulgar, Turkish, Kutzo-Vlach, and Judæo-Spanish, Greek alone is a very inadequate outfit for the military tourist; and I really hardly know which of the extra languages (having due regard to commercial life hereafter) it would be most profitable to study. I have so far formed part of three messes, none of which had a cook; a grievous drawback after life with the French—and of the latest I have just been elected Mess President by acclamation.'
[MAY 3, 1916.]

Patrick Shaw-Stewart.

Xerxes' Country.—To R. A. Knox.
'I am very grateful for the map of Macedonia: it has added several facts to those which I had been trying to piece together, notably the site of Olynthus, and the identification of the Galliko, which had greatly exercised me, and is, of course, the Echedorus (I confess I had not heard of it.) I tried to go to Pella one day, but was frustrated by punctures. This country (I am in the country at present) is a jolly one in spring, and not too hot yet. I am riding an inordinate amount, and (as my saddle is an Army one) acquiring formidable callosities; I should do well in a togger. My modern Greek is beginning to lift its head: I can almost tell a shopman that he is over-charging me by a skilful use of the word περισσός. Don't overdo your Macedonian researches on my account: the periods I want are those prior to Philip and posterior to Alexander; perhaps you could find me a book.'

[MAY 9, 1916.]

To His Sister.
'I have moved, via two or three days in Salonica, to a French Division, which is my old Gallipoli French, who are all very nice, and whom I tend to be happy with, though under-worked. . . . For the rest, the year's at the spring, the day frequently at the morn (or much nearer than I generally see it in time of peace), and the climate at present perfect, we being in the hills; it is true that if we made a masterly advance we should be in the valley of a

Patrick Shaw-Stewart.

river well known to Xerxes and Herodotus, and justly renowned for its mosquitoes, but let us not think of that.' [FOURTH OF JUNE, 1916.]

' If you were a reader of Herodotus I might talk of the place where Xerxes' camels were attacked by lions, and where his army drank one river dry among several named: Ronald would tell you that, if you asked him, and, indeed, one might even perhaps with impunity name the Echedorus, as the name is not exactly in modern use.'
[LIKOVAN, JUNE 7, 1916.]

' I am under a tree which I imagine to be an alder (or possibly a tamarisk), within precisely three feet of the river Echedorus, now shrunk to an inconsiderable brook, which, however, tinkles pleasantly in the moonlight, supplies small fish, which the French cunningly catch and fry, and yields quite a respectable tub if you sit down in it and squish the basin over your head. Only the current is still brisk, and the soap rather liable to be carried downstream, resulting in an undignified chase.'
[KURKUT, JUNE 20, 1916.]

Habits of the French.
' I confess I rather like being in a *house*, and not actually among the insects—though I found a very handsome scarabeus in my bed yesterday, and reproached my servant with it, to which he answered indignantly that I must have brought it in myself

Patrick Shaw-Stewart.

(such a sized thing to bring in without noticing it). I think you asked the other day about him (the servant). He is not my Gallipoli Glasgow body, the W.O. wouldn't let me take him out. This one came to me with my horse when I first came to live with the French six weeks ago. He is rather aged (though hale), a S.A. veteran, reservist of the 10th Hussars, very bright, and not unduly lazy, tho' he likes his little comforts like myself. When he first arrived, or rather two days afterwards, he came to me with an air of tragedy and finality, and said, " I can't eat that French food, sir, I've 'ad nothing but a bit of bread to eat to-day." I pulled myself together and told him severely that French cooking was renowned throughout Europe, and who was he to set himself up against it? " Maybe," he said, " but that there grease they puts into it!" Subsequently he stole several tins of bully beef from a neighbouring British unit, which kept the wolf from the door for a time, and now I think he is becoming slightly more adaptable. He still, however, thirsts for more conversation than he gets with our allies; and constantly hangs about me with openings on the probable duration of the war, or the peculiarities of officers in the 10th Hussars. As you know my theories of the perfect automaton, never more nearly to be realised than in V—— of blessed memory, you can imagine how little encouragement the poor man gets. The horse which accompanied him is a great coarse brute, specially acquired for the original chief *liaison* officer, (who weighed

Patrick Shaw-Stewart.

eighteen stone), with no apparent mouth, but not altogether uncomfortable movements, at least, I've known worse. I've been patiently agitating for another ever since, but, while every one admits my right to it, no one seems inclined to think it over. At present D.S. is at Salonica, and my temporary chief, which quaintly recalls the days when he was Captain of the School.' [JULY 3, 1916.]

To Raymond Asquith.
  ' The only thing I miss is my eggs and bacon; and, after all, when one thinks of what the bacon too often is—— For the rest, I have roamed over Crestonæa and Mygdonia, set foot on the Trans-Strymonic territory of (I think) the Odomanti, encamped by the Echedorus, which Xerxes drained, ranged on the hills where lions attacked his camels, and occasionally looked in on the Thessalonians.' [JUNE 26, 1916.]

  ' I'm just back from three days' continuous riding to do the *liaison* with the nearest British. Rather a lovely journey, the first day all winding among mountain passes, getting up half-way to the *col*, whence you can look down over the flat plain between us and the Bulgars, and up across at the really very handsome heights on which the Bulgars habitually sit: the second day in the plain along a lake with cranes and egrets and little diving ducks all over it. I was tempted to bathe, but a military policeman

Patrick Shaw-Stewart.

whom I came across told me there were five feet of mud, and, anyhow, it was forbidden.'

[KARAMUDLI, JULY, 1916.]

'To-day is the anniversary of something—the taking of the Bastille, I think—and a grateful France supplies a ration of bad champagne to all her brave troops. I have partaken of it, and feel very ill, more that than the heat, I think, which latter is less to-day. It has been pretty hot, always in the nineties, and two days ago it touched 103 in the shade. I didn't know this was such a hot country, nor apparently did any one else. I have changed again, not only my quarters, but my Frenchmen. I am with another division now, which is the only one still in close contact with our army. This time I am in a dirty, dusty little village, half Turk, half gipsy, tucked away in the hills, or rather under them, in case we should lose any benefit of the heat. A British Division in similar circumstances would certainly avoid the village and camp itself in tents outside, thus escaping a certain number of fleas and other little companions, but also suffering a great deal more from heat. The French, on the other hand, who have no illusions about cleanness in time of war, simply choose a few of the least dilapidated houses, and walk in.' [JULY 14, 1916.]

Activity Again.—To Lady Desborough.
'As I told you, about a month ago, I became so bored that I took a step which should have led

Patrick Shaw-Stewart.

eventually to my rejoining the Hood in France; but it has elicited no response whatever, and meanwhile, circumstances have made it unlikely that anything of the kind should go smoothly.'

[AUGUST 7, 1916.]

To His Sister.

' Here, as you will have seen from the papers, we have started a certain liveliness. What the idea is, what we think we are doing, or what the enemy and Rumania intend to do about it, is all Greek to me: my own part in the matter consists of getting up horribly early in the morning, being at the end of a telephone which works exceedingly badly, and is very trying to the nerves, doing a vast deal of office work without the most primitive office appliances such as ink, a table, or a clerk, driving about very dusty roads in a Ford car (distances are generally too great at present for my trusty steeds), and watching picturesque artillery actions from a safe and elegant mountain. In fact, quite a reasonable way of carrying on war compared with many others. Very interesting of course from the tactical and what you may call the minor diplomatic (inter-military) point of view, but so confusing and incomprehensible from the strategic and political as to be sometimes rather irritating. However, I dare say I shall understand when the History of the War comes out. The temperature is very decent now, and we are " under canvas " (I in a tent made by a Spanish Jew of Salonica, named Calderon, a

Patrick Shaw-Stewart.

trade-successor of St Paul, which cost me 200 good drachmas, but is really quite fair) in a little wood on the edge of some hills, much frequented by hoopoes and (I believe they are) pied shrikes. I am now resigned to my third grouseless Autumn (I have already dreed my third English-strawberryless Summer), and can't help thinking the war is getting rather long.' [AUGUST 18, 1916.]

Citation for the Croix de Guerre.
' Le Général Commandant la 17ème Division Coloniale, cité a l'ordre de la Division les officiers dont les noms suivent . . .

' Le capitaine Patrick Houston Shaw-Stewart, officier de liaison attaché a l'Etat-Major de la 17ème Division Coloniale Francaise; officier remarquable, qui a déja rendu a l'Armée Francaise, pendant la Compagne de Dardanelles, des services exceptionnels; décoré de la Legion d'Honneur a ce titre. Vient de se distinguer a nouveau par sa claire intelligence des situations, son activité, ses reconnaissances sous le feu pendant la periode du 9 au 22 Aout, 1916, et a ainsi contribué au succès des attaques Francaises de la 17ème Division Coloniale Francaise.

' Le Général Gerome, Commandant la 17ème Division Coloniale.'
[ENCLOSED IN LETTER, SEPTEMBER 4, 1916.]

Raymond Asquith.—To His Sister.
' I must write to-day so as not to fall into bad habits, but it will be rather a dreary letter, because

Patrick Shaw-Stewart.

I am very miserable about Raymond. I was most awfully fond of him, and admired him, his brain, and his wit, and all his delightful qualities, more than any one else whatever. It makes me more inclined than anything that has happened yet, to "take off my boots and go to bed." Decidedly it's queer—when people like Julian died, you felt at least they had enjoyed war, and were gloriously at home in it: but Raymond! that graceful, elegant cynic, who spent his time before the war pulling Guardsmen's legs, to be killed in action in the Grenadiers, it is so utterly incongruous, and he so completely devoid of any shred of support from glamour. That is what seems to me to make it almost the blackest thing yet—and for me personally there seems to be no man left now, whom I care a brass button for, or he for me, except darling Edward. I *suppose* it's the same for every one: and yet, you know, it's an odd fact that all the people I really cared about are dead, and all the people I used to say "Hallo" to and see when there was nothing better to do are absolutely intact or have had *comfortable* wounds.' [SEPTEMBER 22, 1916.]

To Lady Desborough.
'I selfishly (and I dare say you feel the same) keep turning over in my mind what life will be like without Raymond: and to me just now it seems like an egg without salt. I don't think any one can have loved Raymond more than me, and I'm sure no one can have been such a lickspittle admirer.

Patrick Shaw-Stewart.
I always put him and —— together as the two I knew for my masters; but Raymond was more my master, because I was more frightened of him, and he influenced me in all sorts of ways.'
[OCTOBER 4, 1916.]

Local Feeling.
 ' As for Greece, my one anxiety now is that we may waste time and energy persuading or bullying them into coming in; if they do, they add nothing to our strength, and they constitute another beastly obligation at the end. Whereas, if they remain in our bad books, we can use chunks of their territory to placate the Good Boys afterwards. In my humble opinion, the same thing tends to apply to the Macedonian Revolution that we're all encouraging now—but as the great ones approve of it, I expect it's all all right. A comic development of that has just occurred at ——, not far from here. The inhabitants mistook an allied brigade on the march (which they woke up in the morning and saw camped round them) for a force come to strafe them. They immediately repented of their sins, proclaimed the revolution with shouts of joy, hoisted blue and white armlets, turned out all the gendarmes, the subprefect, and even the Bishop (who was suspected of Tinoism), and went in deputation to express their fidelity and gratitude to the Allied Brigadier, who was deeply touched, but just packing up to move on again.' [SEPTEMBER 22, 1916.]

Patrick Shaw-Stewart.
The Minor Discomforts.—To His Nurse.
'I have been a dreadfully long time without so much as acknowledging your lovely jam, which was greatly appreciated by the French General and me, and the stocking puttees, which are *most* acceptable, after all their travels, as it's getting chilly now, and my old ones are not fit to be seen. Personally, I have nothing to complain of: far enough from the firing line to be completely immune, and near enough to look interesting (to those who don't know)—the house not quite so good, perhaps, as our last, which I was very sorry to leave, but still quite respectable, the only drawbacks being rats, draughts, and sandflies (and a few centipedes). I am trying to coax a very attractive pale yellow cat (who lives in the ruins of the village) to come and live with us and deal with the rats—the draughts only matter when it blows (which it's been doing for three days), and the sandflies are getting rather peaky and pining now the summer is over. Once again I've finished a particularly hot Mediterranean Summer under not very ideal conditions, without having *anything* the matter with me (I don't count one or two odd days), which really, I think, does credit to my constitution and especially to your upbringing. Funny thing you know, Dear, I always used secretly to think you made me put on too many clothes, and that consequently I should lack " resistance " in later life—but the result is that I have developed (apparently) a constitution supremely adapted to campaigning in treacherous climates, and an inside like an emu.' [OCTOBER 3, 1916.]

Patrick Shaw-Stewart.
Efforts to Return.—To Lady Desborough.

'I am thinking again and again of the old original R.N.D. and my lost naval glories. But don't believe this too much, still less tell any one, because I have not yet abandoned my great War principle of the line of least resistance, and few things look more foolish in time of war than a man who talks about rejoining his regiment, but seems in no great hurry to do it.'

[OCTOBER 4, 1916.]

'The weather has been delicious here lately. I have had several afternoons among the partridges. I had two days in Salonica last week, and extravagantly invested in a 200-drachma gun: but I am worse off than before, for a lying thief of a Greek sold me a hundred cartridges loaded with *buckshot*, which he labelled partly "No. 5," and partly "No. 8," damn him: after missing several partridges I have now discovered the fraud by gutting a specimen cartridge; wait till I get him with the Provost Marshal. Meanwhile, I have shot a quail (my first) with one of the buckshot cartridges, probably a record, I should say. On the face of it, I look like being here till all's blue: but something tells me that I might conceivably find myself in England (at any rate for a few days) before the Winter's out. One never knows, you know.'

[HIRSOVA, OCTOBER 22, 1916.]

'Please don't advertise my citation more than you can help; on the one hand, because every one

Patrick Shaw-Stewart.

knows that it is (bless it!) fifty times more an Iron Cross than the Iron Cross, and on the other, because *liaison* officers are in such terribly good a position for getting these things; the French army gives them more as a compliment to the British army than as a distinction to the individual, and, unless the latter is exceptionally humble about them, you run up against the very strong and very justified feeling of those much more combatant, but much less well placed.' [NOVEMBER 4, 1916.]

To His Sister.

'Just two words (because David Scott is going home) to explain my second cable, sent to-day. When I cabled before and even when I wrote, there seemed no obstacle to my going home, except the possibility of my having to replace Scott, but that was got over, and as the *liaison* now seemed clearly superfluous, the obvious thing seemed to be to apply to return to the R.N.D., which I did, with full expectation of its going through: with leave first, of course. No sooner had I done it than I met my Chief, who said, "It's almost certain to be refused." Next thing, I discovered that the Chief of Staff wanted me to come on the Army Staff (Operations) here. I said politely but firmly that I didn't want to, and I have fought it for three days, but no good. They simply will not let me go to France: so the only thing to do is to be good and tame and get leave as soon as I can. These soldiers, poor innocents, cannot get it out of their heads that

Patrick Shaw-Stewart.

I ought to jump at a thing " so good for my career," and it's difficult to say to them that I don't care two kicks on the behind for my career in the damned old Army. Anyhow, there it is—I am set down, from to-morrow, to sticking pins into a map, from eight to one, two to seven, and nine-fifteen to eleven. God help me. Do pity me, I am ashamed and annoyed; annoyed childishly, most of all at not getting home when I had made sure of it—and on the best authority. Anyhow, you may certainly feel I am SAFE here: just a shade safer than I should be in the War Office, and several shades more bored and disgusted.' [NOVEMBER 10, 1916.]

To Lady Desborough.

' My Chief told me he didn't need me with the French Army after all, so I popped in my application to " rejoin my unit." (He had twice told me it was certain to be granted.) In the afternoon he met me and said, " It's almost certain not to be granted," but wouldn't explain. That night he told me why it was: the Chief of Staff wanted me to come on the Army Staff (Operations) here, to replace some one who is leaving. I told him I didn't want that. He told me I should be a fool to refuse it, and it would only mean a row, and anyhow, he was sure the C.-in-C. wouldn't let me go to France. (On my pumping him, it appeared that Amery had put it into the Chief of Staff's head.) We had the usual argument, and I said I was infinitely obliged and flattered, but should certainly

Patrick Shaw-Stewart.

tell the C.G.S. that I didn't want it. Next morning I saw the C.G.S. He said the same sort of things, and made me the offer. I said, " Would you think it insufferable if I asked you to let my application go before the C.-in-C. ? " He said, " I will, if you like, but you're a very perverse fellow." Next day (yesterday) I got a refusal in form. I then asked if I could see the C.-in-C. about it: he said he wouldn't advise me to, so I gave that up. Finally he said I could in no case go to France: but I might go to a battalion here if I insisted! There, of course, he had me, because that I certainly don't want to do. Being killed in France, after a nice leave in London, and in the Hood with my old friends and my old status, is one thing: being killed chillily on the Struma after being pitchforked into God knows what Welsh Fusiliers or East Lancs Regiment is quite another. But of course technically it's illogical of me. Anyhow, I saw that I was done, and accepted the Army Staff, with the full intention of taking leave on the first opportunity (which oughtn't to be very long), and, once in London, of course the thing's as simple as winking: or perhaps not quite as simple as I think, but certainly doable. Meanwhile, to-morrow I begin my gruesome bottle-washing duties in a God-forsaken office in this blasted town. No doubt I shall make, with my City training, a very fair confidential clerk; and no doubt that's what they think, damn them.

'PS.—Of course none of these soldiers can

Patrick Shaw-Stewart.

quite get it out of their heads that I must be mad not to jump at a thing "so good for my career," poor innocents.' [NOVEMBER 10, 1916.]

New Quarters.
 ' It is a really magnificent villa, built for Prince Andrew, but now belonging to an enemy Turk, so we have no scruples about violating the furniture. It is quite hideous, with a superstructure like the Taj, but clean (the first time I have seen a clean house in Macedonia) and with doors that shut. The inhabitants at present are the senior chaplain (I don't know to what extent he will cramp one's style: he talks very sportingly about "selling one pups" and things, so perhaps one might try a little anecdote on him to see), a barrister called Cohen, who runs the Claims, Amery, the anti-gas expert, and me; but we shall probably swell, because the house is so attractive. It is, by the way, right *in* the sea.' [NOVEMBER 29, 1916.]

Foss Prior.—To Mrs Prior.
 ' Every one loved, and (I would almost say) looked up to Foss at school; he had so greatly the qualities of leadership; self-possession, will-power, readiness and sureness, besides being good at games. I remember how greatly I envied those qualities of his in early years, when I was rather a timid and sometimes lonely little boy myself. But besides the qualities which made for popularity at school (and at Oxford, if possible, win more), he

Patrick Shaw-Stewart.

had those which make and keep friends, he was so good-natured, so kind, so interested in people and things, and above all so loyal, and so absolutely straightforward. I always think he must have been about the best Captain of the School that ever was, and that I did Eton a good turn by making way for him.

'I am sorry to think how much less I saw of Foss at Oxford, of course it was inevitable, because colleges are colleges, and I was very Balliol, and he was the very centre of University. We used to amuse each other by saying that we couldn't live in each other's colleges. Certainly University suited Foss admirably: he was loved at Eton, and he " ran " them, as he had " run " College, in his quiet, capable, irresistible way.

'It is a very early and precious piece of my life which seems to have gone with Foss, and which catches at my heart among the deaths of my friends, which seem now to come every day.'

[NOVEMBER, 1916.]

Monastir.
' I spent a week in Monastir the other day. The chief difficulty was getting there: I tried to go by Ford car, but (encouraged by a Serb captain) I drove straight into a lake which at one point had invaded the road, and my chauffeur, my servant, and I, had to take off practically all our clothes, tuck up our shirts under our arms, and shove first 1000 yards forward and then (as it only got deeper)

Patrick Shaw-Stewart.

turn the car by manual labour and shove about 300 yards back again, an indecent spectacle loudly cheered by the Italian army. The car having failed, I had to go that night by the French " trolley," a small open truck propelled by a sort of motor that runs along the railway. It started at one in the morning and took about 10 hours. It was one of the coldest things I ever did: but it was fun waking up in the dawn at Ostrovo and seeing the sun hit Kaimakchalan through the mist: all the country from there on to the Monastir plain is lovely, and the greatest change from Salonica. The Frenchman, Leblois, now commanding the Army up there, was an old friend of mine and was very nice to me. I stayed there four days, and did about half the things I wanted to. Monastir is a jolly-looking town in a lovely situation, with a liberal supply of minarets and broad, infamously cobbled streets. Going in from the South is rather grim, dead horses and enormous shell-holes: that is the end the enemy plug, for the benefit of the station and the road. (They also plug one of the other ends for the benefit of the French artillery, and they speeded it up rather while I was there, but you couldn't say they were exactly bombarding the town.) The population left is about a quarter of the peace time numbers; mostly Turks and Jews, and nearly all the women are veiled. (In contradistinction I saw one French *cocotte* in full panoply walking down a dilapidated street, very odd-looking.) The Jews, who have stayed to look after their shops, are very

Patrick Shaw-Stewart.

neutral; they have barred and bolted their doors heavily, and occasionally one peers through a grating; they are obviously more afraid of being pillaged by us than sacked by the enemy.'

[DECEMBER 20, 1916.]

Mr Britling.

' I grant that for weaker brethren it's dangerous to begin thinking how well we've always behaved to Denmark, and blacks, and Ireland, and so on: but, you know, I really think the weaker brethren ought to try and think a little sometimes, and to any one who ever *does* think, it seems to me a hopeless proposition to try and make either war or peace on the assumption that we are all good and the Germs all bad. After all, we've got to live with them when it's all over. But then, I've got a rottenly equipped mind for conducting a great war, and fortunately it's not me that had to do the conducting. But generally I think you can trust the press to say a book's pro-German if it's within ten miles of being so, and I see Mr Britling has an excellent press. Must stop—go on writing till I cable—I daren't say whether I think I shall get leave soon—Christmas having so failed—but I might.'

The Last of Greece.

' As for Greece, it's simply unspeakable, or rather has been, because I really think we've put the fear of God into them at last. All very well, of course,

Patrick Shaw-Stewart.

to say we ought to have shelled Athens and abducted Tino, but the latter is extremely popular, and it would have been the greatest bore in the world to have Greece going to war with us. I really don't know whether it's worth getting leave nowadays, when I read the papers. Even if one succeeds in getting home without being torpedoed, apparently you can't spend more than four shillings on your dinner, and the few remaining drinks will evidently be cut off soon, and now I see no one is to be allowed to travel by train for Christmas.'

Chapter Nine

THE attempt that had proved so hopeless at Salonica—the attempt to leave his position of comparative security on the Staff, and rejoin his old companions in the Hood Battalion—did not prove too much for Patrick's power of " getting things done," when he returned on leave to England. His health had suffered (as many people's had) by the climate of Macedonia, and by speaking softly to a medical board he managed to have his return there vetoed: this was about the end of February. By April he was already in France with his old battalion, where he served for the rest of the year, with an interval of leave in the early winter shortly before his death. Towards the end of this time he was in temporary command of the battalion. He was killed on the 30th of December.

His letters throughout the war make constant allusions to the effect made on him by the deaths of his contemporaries and friends—old friends like Foss Prior, whom he had known best at Eton and seen little of since Oxford, and new friends like Rupert Brooke, whom he met for the first time as a fellow officer in the Hood. Thus he writes as early as August 25th, 1915 :—

' I wonder if this war has come specially hard on my friends—I suppose not. At first sight it looks

Patrick Shaw-Stewart.

a long list. Denny Anson just before, and then John Manners, Twiggy Anderson, Hoj and the other Fletcher, Volly Heath, Julian and Billy and Douglas, and Rupert and Denis Browne out here, and now Charles is in danger and Edward just out. The fact is that this generation of mine is suffering in their twenties what most men get in their seventies, the gradual thinning out of their contemporaries—do you remember how it used to depress Father? Nowadays we who are alive have the sense of being old, old survivors.'

'By the end of this time at Salonica, Patrick felt that only one of the old fellowship remained in the fighting line—Edward Horner, whom he managed to meet several times while in France, and whose death he heard of when on leave in the winter of 1917. Of his fellow-officers in the Hood, only one is now frequently named in his correspondence.

The impression created by these losses was not, for Patrick, relieved by any certain hope of immortality. I have no desire to discuss his religious outlook in general, the phrase (in a letter of July 24th, 1917), ' I never felt tempted to be an atheist myself, or anything near so committal,' shall stand by itself without comment. But it is certain that the question of immortality worried him—worried him chiefly because others appeared to find it simple, and the independent (I mean, non-religious) evidence which they adduced in favour of their view seemed to him, with his sternly exacting

Patrick Shaw-Stewart.

standard of proof, inadequate evidence. I cannot resist quoting a lonely reference in this connection from his correspondence in 1910, in the shape of a parody of the Shropshire Lad, written in protest against the Pantheistic or semi-Pantheistic doctrine of 'survival':—

'. . . But I distrust your speculations, and feel impelled to reply :—

> ' When *I* feel as brisk as that
> (Which is rare), I'll eat my hat
> If I think that it portends
> Any post-terrestrial ends.
> My pedantic atom-soul
> Will *not* be Part of any Whole,
> And no affinity admits
> With other embryonic chits.
> Absolute quiescence here
> Might indicate a further sphere;
> But all this bustle, sure, implies
> Little left for Stars or Skies.
> Rest my body, rest my soul;
> Hole me at the eighteenth hole. . . .

The date of the composition must be apology for those who lift their brows over its flippancy. Later, during the war, he writes in a more serious vein, but with the same refusal to have his judgment influenced by anything like sentimental considerations.

Patrick Shaw-Stewart.

'I think you have a good war-temperament—sane, humorous, enduring, and pugnacious: only you miss the real mainspring of my phlegm and success in life, which is incuriosity. I am really not exercised about the issues of life and death —was I, five years ago? not much, I think—and am settling down to good solid practical subjects like Political Philosophy and the works of Samuel Butler. Still, I will tell you so much; one thing I am sure of, and one thing makes me angry. I am sure that there is nothing to be looked for from the dead, either by the world in general or by me in particular, for the simple reason that whatever there is or is not, there is manifestly an end of consciousness, of the memories and associations of such and such a mind in such and such a body: and anything short of that is no use to me, or to "this" world. And the thing that makes me angry is that people should lose, gain, intensify, or in any way differentiate their religion or irreligion because (*a*) a great many people have been killed; (*b*) some one they like (1) has been killed, or (2) may be. It isn't the silliness, if you take me, so much as the stupidity that I mind. Now on this delicate subject (delicate because it's no use treading on the toes of people who've just lost their lover or their son), you seem to me to begin admirably (though I rather suspect your peace-time Nature-worship, reserved, as you state it, for great occasions), but to tail off badly into a weak attitude on the Mons question (on which you seem to me to resemble an

Patrick Shaw-Stewart.

excellent top-hat Christian who once told me she had no objection to saying the Apostles' Creed, because what it really meant was that self-sacrifice is beautiful), and worse still on the postures of the dead. Accept a little first-hand evidence from a poor devil of a *piou-piou* (who sees much more of the dead than the gunners do) like myself, who assure you the phenomenon has entirely escaped my notice. I have seen them in all sorts of queer positions, probably having been in pain at the time of their dissolution, but never remarked the prayerful attitude, nor the Turks (for that matter) turned towards Mecca.' [NOVEMBER 7, 1915.]

To the last, as far as we know, his attitude was one of not being able to share his friends' confidence, and 'wondering' whether he would ever find himself able to do so.

The feeling of loneliness in relation to his own circle was combined, I think, with a certain flatness of general outlook towards the end of Patrick's life. Those of us who have good memories for recording past impressions will agree that 1917 was the most dispiriting period of the war; we had lost most of our old illusions, and the time had not yet come when we were to draw our breath and then sigh it out again in relief at the tidings of victory. We all tended to live more for the moment, to clutch at the creature comforts that were vanishing from our tables, to ask forgetfulness. The grip had not relaxed, but the effort was only half conscious, half

Patrick Shaw-Stewart.

muscular reaction. In France itself, hopes were less buoyant among the troops, and doggedness had to replace the will to victory. Something of this staleness reflects itself in Patrick's correspondence: the letters are apparently fewer in number, and their laughter is more forced, their weariness more apt to show through. True, he was closer to English life and congenial society, but the emptiness is there. Characteristically, too, he had doubts of his own capacity for important regimental commands at a time when outside critics agreed that he was sustaining them admirably. Of description, in any detail, at any rate, of the country he was fighting in and the actions in which he was concerned there is far less than formerly, but probably here he felt that the ground had been too well covered by others to allow of fresh treatment. The following extracts, then, will hardly be more than a brief record of his movements.

. . .

Working the Oracle.

‘ This is the situation. After I got the Salonica answer to the W.O. refusing to release me, I thought it was finished. But after talking to the R.N.D. people, I thought I might play my inside. I really don't know whether I was right, but I did feel a strong impulse to do everything to avoid going back to that absurd Salonica. So I got —— to put my troubles (quite real ones) on paper, and applied to the W.O. for a Medical Board. This has now been granted, but they haven't named a day, only ordered

Patrick Shaw-Stewart.

me to wait here in the meantime. So everything depends on the Board. If they say there's not much the matter with me I shall go to Salonica after all: if they say I'm not fit for the East they will (I suppose) pass me fit for general service barring that, and then I shall be able to get back to the R.N.D. I hope you don't think it's silly or perverse of me: you know I've wanted to go back for some time. [LONDON, FEBRUARY 24, 1917.]

' I have had my Board yesterday morning, and they passed me for General Service with the recommendation that I should not be sent back to the East. That was my own suggestion: they would quite certainly have passed me for anything I jolly well liked. That being so, I shall in a day or two probably be informed of it officially by the W.O., whereupon I will communicate with Freyberg, who will apply for me. It will all take some time probably: nothing is done in a hurry in the British Army.

'Please don't be perturbed about my inside. It is very well indeed, and in this country (and presumably in France), I should never give it a thought. In Gallipoli, and places like that, of course it has been occasionally dickey with little goes of " dysentery " and jaundice and what not, but nothing to what most people have out here, and nothing which would have been worth mentioning, except with an ulterior object. I feel more and more that I have been right to play my last card to

Patrick Shaw-Stewart.

get out of Salonica and back to France. In fact, I think I have conducted the personal problem of this war with exceptional felicity, and made the best of both worlds. Please try and agree with me; but I shall get a lecture from Basil.'

[OXFORD, MARCH 3, 1917.]

A Course at Le Touquet.
 ' I'm well embarked on the Course at the Depot here. I can't honestly say I think it's teaching me very much I haven't known by heart these three years back, except, perhaps, a little about gas and bomb-throwing: but there is a terrible lot of indifferent lecturing out of books and old-fashioned sloping of arms, which I really thought I had undergone once for all at the Crystal Palace. No doubt it is extremely good for the soul of a veteran like me to be marched about in fours and told to be in by 9 p.m., but occasionally one is tempted to forget how comic it all is, and also how tolerable. For it really is exceedingly tolerable, if measured by the discomforts that are always possible; I have my bed, I have a tent to myself, a very respectable mess, and a great stand-by in the shape of the Sutherland Hospital, which is at a reasonable distance. I have dined there twice, and do it again to-night. The only drawback is that after being marched about and bored to death from 8.20 to 4.15, one is rather inclined to sink into a chair and drop into a hoggish sleep, more than to brush one's hair nicely and walk

Patrick Shaw-Stewart.

another mile to a tram—or, indeed, to write letters or any other elegant occupation.'

[LE TOUQUET, APRIL 24, 1917.]

Hospital Visits.—To Millicent, Duchess of Sutherland.
'You can't imagine how wonderful it was for me to be dumped in that particular camp for a fortnight, within striking distance of your enchanted hospital. Never did a Lonely Soldier have such phenomenal luck. It would have reconciled —— himself to being absent from the battalion for a few days. You were an angel to let me come so often and take so many meals and baths off you. (I would give a lot for one of them now.) It only remains to acquire as quickly as possible a wound of the right degree of gravity and return as a patient. It took me about three days to get to the battalion, and I've been with it a week. It has been very much " in " and done very well—just the time they were keeping me at Calais—and now ought (we think) to be resting, but instead is working hard just behind the line.'

[MAY 15, 1917.]

The Front.
'Don't entertain any ill-grounded hopes (or apprehensions) if my kit-bag turns up labelled "Officer's Kit," that being the only label I could find. They made us reduce our kit, but some things in it might perhaps be judiciously sent back, also a bulky book called *The Idea of God*, which K. will no doubt devour meanwhile. I'll write later about that. Since I last wrote there has been no change

Patrick Shaw-Stewart.

in our position or occupation (except that by careful arrangement I am now spending far more of my nights in bed), or, for that matter, in our immediate prospects. Having now actually inhabited the same place for a fortnight, the battalion is beginning to make itself reasonably comfortable. We most of us inhabit old Boche dug-outs of the real picture-paper kind, incredibly deep, and really wonderfully spacious, dug-outs in which the gentle German obviously intended to pass the remainder of his days, while missiles from B. and such like fell harmlessly over his head. Personally, I get claustrophobia in these dungeons, and so inhabit a bivouac with my second in command, though the last few nights I have slightly doubted my wisdom, since the weather has broken. However, I haven't actually been flooded yet: and am triumphantly sticking to my bed, the wise O.C. having ordained that each " Company Headquarters " may possess a bed and a bath. It just shows how prudent it is to travel as *heavy* as possible till you are gradually stripped, and then buy a new lot—my principle, I'm glad to say, since the beginning of hostilities. I wish the weather would get really nice and hot; I thought it had settled to, but it hadn't. It's very noisy on this front, even when you're not in immediate proximity to the guns: noisier, I think, than anything I ever heard. But then one's heard so much about it from W. Beach Thomas that one isn't in the least surprised. Could you get me this week's *Penny Pictorial*, containing H. G. Wells on the

Patrick Shaw-Stewart.

Future of Monarchy ? By the way, I have of course ordered his new book about God, and we shall probably disagree violently about it.'
[MAY 18, 1917.]

' I've been second in command of the battalion till a day or two ago, when a very jolly man called Mark Egerton came back and took it over, so now I'm next to him. The battalion haven't really had a proper rest yet since the time in April before I rejoined when they were very busy, and I think they ought to get it soon. However, at present they really haven't much to complain of, being used for odd jobs behind the line—we're now in very comfortable tin huts—before, we were in rather smelly old Boche dug-outs, which I refused to live in, and pitched my tent outside. It rained a bit in those days, and when I went down the men's dug-outs to inspect them, I generally did the last ten steps in a sitting position.' [MAY 27, 1917.]

' They say leave conditions are greatly improving in the B.E.F., and, indeed, I have just packed off ten dreamy-looking A.B.'s all wreathed in smiles. A funny thing has just happened to me, they sent an order yesterday, that while we were out they wanted all Company Commanders to go in succession for three days to an Artillery Brigade and live with them, so that we foot-sloggers might get some notions of the fine art in our thick skulls, and not be so unreasonable in asking for support, and

Patrick Shaw-Stewart.

complaining of short shelling. I, being O.C. "A" Company, was despatched forthwith and reported to a neighbouring Artillery Brigade. This turned out to be commanded by the ex-padre who ejected Basil at Suvla, apparently he loves Basil dearly, so he fell on my neck and brought out his one bottle of whisky. (Fortunately, I remembered he was an ex-padre, so confined myself to drawing-room anecdotes.) This morning he has sent me up to a Battery, but insists I am to come back to sleep with him each night. So useful is it to have an eminent brother. The battery commander is out, so I am lying flat on my tummy in the grass outside his habitat in the amiable sun, waiting till he comes in; one of the pleasanter phases of war. When I have written to you, and X, and Y, and Z, I will go on with *Tom Jones*, which I am in the middle of, and which is far and away the best book I ever read. Messrs Meredith and James are simply silly beside it, and as for the Victorians ———. I got through *Sense and Sensibility* the other day, by the way, not bad, but not half as good as *Pride and Prejudice*, or *Emma*.'

'I did tell you about our time up the line? It was quite agreeable, good weather (though a lot of mud), and a quiet time, very few casualties. I had rather luck having a chain of posts very much advanced in a rather well-known place, so far advanced as to be clear of mud and also clear of shelling. The only trial was that I hardly got a wink of sleep—one has to re-acquire the habit of

Patrick Shaw-Stewart.

sleeping in a sitting-position on a petrol tin in the later half of the morning. Since we've been down again, they keep shifting us about, apparently because they can't make up their mind which rearward defences they want us to work on. I wish they would hurry up, because in each camp I make a beautiful Company Mess, and then immediately we move out.' [GAVRELLE ROAD, JUNE 11, 1917.]

A Lewis Gun Course.
'I need hardly say that I provide many hearty laughs for my school-fellows, as always occurs when poor Pady has to deal with the tiresome *mechanics* incidental to modern war. I wish I had lived in the flint-head-arrow period; I could have instructed a company much better in them.'
[JULY 4, 1917.]

In Command.
'In a great hustle because Oc. has gone on leave, and Mark Egerton is going to Artillery for three days and I have to command the Hood Battalion! Lord bless my soul! I hope there won't be any crises. Yesterday I arose (for the second time) from a bed of very little sickness, diagnosed as mild trench-fever—even the friendliest doctor couldn't give me a temp. of more than 100.2 the second go, and now I have no more excuse for bed. We are going into reserve for a few days, which fulfils my military ideal of No Fighting and No Training, but which may be rather overcrowded. I may get

Patrick Shaw-Stewart.

leave to Paris any day now—but (irony) the trouble now is to get a companion; will write properly soon.' [ROCLINCOURT, JULY 29, 1917.]

To Lady Hermione Buxton.
'I am not a very good regimental officer, and, to tell you the honest, I don't enjoy it overmuch. You don't get as much leisure when out of the line as you did in Gallipoli: too much damned training, which (next to fighting) I dislike more than anything. However, my views on life as affected by the war are not quite so sombre as yours: every time I remember that nearly all my friends are dead, I take some form of imaginary morphia, and promise myself work or love or letters, or fall back on the comforting reflection that I may soon be dead myself (wonderfully cheering, that).'
[JULY 30, 1917.]

To His Sister.
'It was a strange sensation to find myself commanding the old battalion—it just shows what we are all reduced to nowadays; I should think old Quilter would turn in his grave to contemplate the prospect.' [AUGUST 8, 1917.]

Comforts.
'Honey and oatcakes sound absolutely perfect, only I don't want to eat up all the food supply of the Kessock district. But oatcakes would be a

Patrick Shaw-Stewart.

lovely change—could they be *thin*, please? because my teeth are getting feebler and feebler as I get older and older. (I shall be 29 in a few days, isn't it an age?) We have been up and down lately in a peaceful sector, worlds away from the offensive; it looks as if we were going to be left to hold the line here when everybody else has gone north to fight. I'm hoping to get three or four days in Paris soon, but I find it difficult to arrange to go with any one from another regiment, because we all get leave thrown at our heads, " take it or leave it," at different times. The weather is beastly, raining nearly every day: I'm living in a deep dug-out which doesn't mind rain, but my mess is on a chalk slope, and has alarming landslips every day. I know the roof will be down before it's finished.'

[AUGUST 12, 1917.]

International Politics.

' I have completely lost myself in the Stockholm controversy, can no longer remember who wants to go there and who doesn't, and from constantly striving to disagree with both the *Times* and the *Nation*, can no longer even remember what I want myself. (The British Army, by the way, is solid for Stockholm.) As for the Russians and Riga . . . and Flanders seems to have gone completely to sleep; not that I mind that much; nasty muddy place, I hope they don't send me there.'

[SEPTEMBER 7, 1917.]

Patrick Shaw-Stewart.
The Company Commanders' Course.

'Three days ago, I was sent here to the Army School to do the Company Commanders' course: rather suddenly, because my second in command was to have gone, and at the last moment they said they must have a real Company Commander, and I was the only one sufficiently badly educated to send. So I was packed off, and after a more than usually uncomfortable journey, fetched up here last night. No harm, I imagine, in saying that the School is in the famous Chateau d'Hardelot. The two remarkable points about it are (1) that it's a lovely place (though restored from top to bottom), and in a lovely half-wooded valley with the sea the other side of the ridge; (2) that this is the place where the Duchess of Rutland tried to have a hospital—I never realised till I got here how complete the preparations were. I toiled up last night to try and draw a blanket and sheet. No, I am not billeted inside the chateau, but in a neat hut behind it; and the unfeeling lance-corporal in charge of the blankets said, "No, sir: these blankets are the private property of the Duchess of Rutland, and can only be issued to officers *in* the chateau." The temptation was almost irresistible to explain that I knew she would be *delighted* to let *me* have one, but I kind of felt that the lance-corporal had been told that too often; so I meekly toddled off to draw an Army blanket off the Quartermaster several miles away. To-day has not been strenuous, consisting mostly of roll-calls: to-morrow the course

Patrick Shaw-Stewart.

begins. What exactly they propose to teach me, I scarcely know, but apparently forming fours is an important part of it. Anyhow, it lasts five weeks, so you have no excuse for thinking of me as fighting battles during that period; and by that time I should be over-ripe for leave. The officers (innumerable) on this course are very like most modern representatives of their class: the nicest are the Canadians and Americans (we have a batch of them), which two nations have, in their wisdom, seen fit to amalgamate the upper and middle classes in one, an arrangement by which, if you miss the former, you also (which is more important in the Army) miss the other.' [SEPTEMBER 30, 1917.]

In Command Again.
 ' Meanwhile, Oc..Asquith has gone on leave and left me in command, by Jove! No nonsense from the junior officers, I can tell you. My first action was to put myself in for immediate promotion to Lieutenant-Commander, sound, don't you think? My second, to place a man who has just arrived from spending three years in England, more or less, and who is senior, not only to all my company commanders, but to myself, handsomely —to place him, I say, *second in command of a company*.' [NOVEMBER 13, 1917.]

Back from Leave.
 ' Thank you for your letter, which I got the last morning. As I telegraphed, I sailed on Wed.

Patrick Shaw-Stewart.

morning, or rather, afternoon. By virtue of being a Major (by Jove!), I went on the Staff train at 12.50, comfortable-like, instead of having to push off at 7 a.m. I had a lovely crossing, followed by a considerable surprise: expecting to find the battalion roughly where I had left them, I found that they had gone almost as far from there as they could—and for the last forty-eight hours I have been trying to catch them up, so far with very little success. I have been in about a dozen trains, all smelly, and subsisted largely on chocolate and apples. I hope I will fetch up soon.'

· · · · · ·

The following letter from Lord Alexander Thynne gives the circumstances of Patrick's death circumstantially enough to need no amplification :

' By a curious coincidence, two days ago, I had as artillery *liaison* officer the man who was actually with Patrick Shaw-Stewart when he was killed, in the next sector. It was an exceptionally gallant death. It was in the early morning, about dawn; he was going round his line; the Germans put up a barrage. The gunner pressed him to send up the S.O.S. rocket, but Patrick refused, and maintained that it was only a minor raid on another part of the line, and that if he sent up the S.O.S. signal the people would only think he was " windy." As a matter of fact, they did make a big attack about an hour later, and his battalion was the only one that did not give ground.

' He was hit by shrapnel, the lobe of his ear was

Patrick Shaw-Stewart.

cut off and his face spattered so that the blood ran down from his forehead and blinded him for a bit. The gunner tried to make him go back to Battalion H.Q. to be dressed, but he refused, and insisted on completing his round. Very soon afterwards, a shell burst on the parapet, and a fragment hit him upwards through the mouth and killed him instantaneously. This gunner, who was in the ranks of the R.F.A. before the war, and as *liaison* officer with the infantry can speak with sure experience, says that he has never seen a battalion better organised. He was intensely struck with Patrick's capacity; there was no detail to do with the men's comfort to which he did not give the closest personal attention. And he spoke with the greatest admiration of his fearless personal courage. He mentioned all this in the course of ordinary conversation, without being aware that I knew him at all well.

'His battalion fought well; they seem to have been a fine lot, with a splendid fighting spirit. I thought this might interest you. It was very pleasant to hear, for, whatever the grief may be at home, a death like this is so undoubtedly worth while.'

GLASGOW: W. COLLINS SONS AND CO. LTD.

HISTORY OF ENGLISH FURNITURE
By Percy Macquoid, R.I.

With plates in colour after Shirley Slocombe, and numerous illustrations selected and arranged by the author; in four volumes: I.—*The Age of Oak*; II.—*The Age of Walnut*; III.—*The Age of Mahogany*; IV.—*The Age of Satin Wood*. £10 10s. per set or £2 12s. 6d. per volume. Size, 15" × 11"; bound in red buckram, gilt.

By arrangement with Messrs Lawrence and Bullen, who first issued the book, Messrs Collins will now continue its publication.

MR MACQUOID'S book is so greatly valued among amateurs and collectors that it may justly be said that it is the standard work on English furniture. As a book of reference alone, it holds an unequalled position owing to the very large number of illustrations of the finest pieces in the country.

For the benefit of those to whom the book is unfamiliar a word as to its arrangement may be given.

The subject has been divided into four periods, the first dating from 1500 to 1660, comprising furniture that can be attributed to the Renaissance, and its evolution from the Gothic. The second from 1660 to 1720, when the change is varied by the Restoration and Dutch influence, followed by a distinctly assertive English spirit. The third period covers the introduction from France of fresh ideas in design, clearly marking another change, lasting from 1720 to 1770. The fourth, 1770–1820, which was inspired by an affectation for all things classical. While the book only purports to deal with English furniture, it is obvious that reference is freely made to foreign styles in order to keep the matter in perspective.

The plates in this book were all specially taken under the author's direction, and are so selected as to show the best work in detail of the finest pieces in England. They number some 1000 in addition to the coloured plates prepared from watercolour drawings.

It is a book that should be in every house in Great Britain where beautiful things are treasured, and, moreover, is of undoubtedly immense value to furniture dealers, designers, and architects

Collins' Spring List   *1920*

HARVEST
By Mrs Humphry Ward
Author of *Cousin Philip*, etc.   7s. 6d. net

THIS story of a charming woman is in Mrs Ward's most admirable vein, and is a love story such as perhaps only she knows how to tell. Rachel leaves a wreck of a life behind her and takes to farming. In the rather sleepy countryside this is not unattended by difficulties or humours, but, while these form the surface of her life, the past stalks grimly behind. She falls in love with a young American officer, whose character has given Mrs Ward one of her great opportunities. How these two lay the ghost of the past is the thread of this novel, which is a fine rounded book handled in a masterly fashion.

THE TALL VILLA
By Lucas Malet
Author of *Sir Richard Calmady, Deadham Hard*, etc.   7s. 6d. net

A NEW book by Lucas Malet needs no introduction to the public. From the days of *Sir Richard Calmady* and the *Wages of Sin*, she has kept her place among the leading group of novelists of the time. Suffice it, then, to say that to give even a glimpse of this story to which the much abused adjective 'thrilling' may justly be applied, would be to lift the curtain on a mystery the possibilities and probabilities of which are much mooted in general just now.

DENYS THE DREAMER
By Katharine Tynan
Author of *The Man from Australia*, etc.   7s. 6d. net

A STORY of an Irish lad whose dreams for once are not of frail stuff. It is a romantic book, written with all this author's happy certainty of touch, and one which will make a definite mark. The pictures of Ireland and Irish life which form the running, though not continuous background of the story, are soft and harsh by turns, reflecting every mood and change of that wonderful, puzzling country.

Collins' Spring List   **1920**

THE CHEATS: A Romantic Phantasy
By Marjorie Bowen
Author of *Mr Misfortunate*, etc.   7s. 6d. *net*

THE author of this tale of intrigue may justly claim to be the novelist of the 'costume' period *par excellence*. It would certainly be difficult to find a book fuller of the subtlety of the Jacobean Jesuit, of plot and counterplot, court scandal, and subterranean politics. Her atmosphere is to a degree perfect, that the reader, absorbed in the period, is tempted to forget the modern novelist behind, with her penetrating interest in the hidden character of the players, and to read for the story alone.

MARY-GIRL
By Hope Merrick   7s. *net*

A DRAMATIC and powerful story of a man with a passionate belief in the righteousness of his objective, a belief that comes near to wrecking not only all his own happiness, but the life of a wife to whom he is devoted. The cataclysm in which he sees his man-made ideal shattered brings a tense, poignant situation at the end of a story that leads the reader artistically forward through many of the rough places of human existence.

THE BANNER
By Hugh F. Spender
Author of *The Seekers*   7s. *net*

'A FIT place for heroes to live in'—this phrase rings through Mr Spender's new book, in which Helen Hart and her League of Youth abolish the old order. How many of us have had a vision of that new England in which youth is to play the dominant part? Mr Spender crystallises that vision with freshness, humour, and sincerity. The story rings true, and the reality is wonderfully maintained. He has not neglected human nature, and with a skill that is remarkable in a novel in which 'politics'—or what replaces them—are the main theme, he avoids the temptation to preach. It is a book that brims over with youth, cheerful, lively and full of zest.

AN IMPERFECT MOTHER
By J. D. Beresford
Author of *God's Counterpoint*, etc. 7s. 6d. net

MR BERESFORD'S last novel, *The Jervaise Comedy*, was in a lighter vein than his earlier work, but in this book he returns to his more serious manner. The main object is the portraiture of a mother and her son, but with characteristic skill Mr Beresford, in painting his portraits, makes his figures sit well into their frame. They fit their background, and there is a solidity in every person in the book quite distinctively unusual. It has not sufficed him to sketch shadowy 'characters' —they are rather 'the people in the play,' nor is it too much to say that the author has never achieved a finer book.

POTTERISM
By Rose Macaulay
Author of *What Not*, *Non-Combatants*, etc. 7s. 6d. net

MISS MACAULAY'S witty, satirical vein was by no means exhausted by her clever study, in *What Not*, of a Government Department. In her new book she, little by little, extends her humorous comments on Society until she includes the whole of English life of to-day. She has, however, in doing this portrayed a vivid and intensely human group of characters. Jane Potter may well stand as the final portrait of present-day young womanhood. You should also make the acquaintance of John Potter, Clare Potter, and Potters *père et mère*.

PANDORA'S YOUNG MEN
By Frederick Watson
Author of *The Humphries Touch* 7s. 6d. net

NO one who read about the inimitable Humphries will hesitate a moment to see what Mr Watson offers next. He has in his humour some of the subtlety of an Anstey, but it is gayer, more human. This book is a modern comedy of manners on a wider stage than before, but written in the same vein in its attitude towards the official, social, and provincial society of to-day.

THE FOOLISH LOVERS
By St. John Ervine
Author of *Changing Winds*, *Mrs Martin's Man*, etc. 7s. 6d. net

FOR some years the literary world has been watching Mr Ervine. His progressive steps up the ladder have been steady and sure, for he has in him all the qualities that lead to success in literature. The interest, therefore, of his new book will lie partly in the estimating of a further creative step towards that position which we feel sure is Mr Ervine's destiny. The author's fine, narrative style will be seen at its best in this new novel, which traces the career of a young Belfast man.

ADAM OF DUBLIN: A Romance of To-day
By Conal O'Riordan ('Norreys Connell')
Author of *The Young Days of Admiral Quilliam*, etc. 7s. 6d. net

THE author of this novel has, from time to time, as his somewhat infrequent books have appeared, earned praise that was never faint from the leading critics of the day. Wells, Shaw, Conrad, Zangwill, Edward Thomas, Henry Davray, have testified in turn to his humour, his graceful wit, his sincerity of observation. He is one of the rare authors who have published too few books. Unfortunately the stage, the Abbey Theatre, Dublin, has occupied too much of his time. He has been called by more than one critic, a genius. It is certain that no other writer could have created *Adam of Dublin*, with its firmly humane and even exalted handling of scenes which a lesser man might make simply painful. But it is the delicious humour, the palpitating vigour of this picture of Dublin to-day, of all ranks of society as seen through the eyes of a child raised from the gutter, that makes the primary appeal of the novel.

CHALLENGE
By V. Sackville-West (Hon. Mrs Harold Nicolson)
Author of *Heritage* 7s. 6d. net

ALL the glamour and brilliant sunshine of the Mediterranean illuminates this author's second novel, in which she describes in her own finished manner a revolution in the Greek Islands. The period of the story is the twentieth century, and the dominating figures are the young Englishman and his passionate, beautiful cousin Eve.

SIR HARRY
By Archibald Marshall
Author of *The Graftons*, etc.   7s. 6d. *net*

THE young man who gives the name to this book is perhaps one of the most sympathetic characters ever presented by Mr Marshall. His upbringing, so full of reserves, so unlike that of the typical schoolboy, yet produces a human being instinct with the best of English qualities, with a thoughtful, simple side to it that has never been more successfully developed by any of our modern novelists. Mr Marshall, as usual, displays a wonderful mastery of his subject.

THE CLINTONS AND OTHERS
By Archibald Marshall
Author of *The Graftons*, etc.   7s. *net*

CONTAINS two stories about the Clinton family, who have appeared in several of Mr Marshall's novels. The first tells of the way in which Merchant Jack rescued the estate of Kencote from the hands of his spendthrift brother, 'Beau' Clinton; the other is a long story which recounts the effects of the war upon the Clintons who took part in it, and especially upon the Squire.

Four other stories make up the book. The two longer ones are 'In That State of Life,' which deals with the courtship of Lord Kimmeridge, an eminent scientist, and 'Audacious Ann,' in which a high-spirited and amusing child fights a whole school single-handed to shield an absent schoolfellow, who had committed an offence of which she herself was accused.

THE SWORD OF LOVE
By Moray Dalton
Author of *Olive in Italy*   7s. *net*

THIS is a romance of Italy in the golden days of the revival of art and learning. It tells how Marco Landi, going in search of his little half-sister Fiore, came to the Court of Lorenzo The Magnificent and was involved in the tragic adventure of the Pazzi Conspiracy.

THE DARK RIVER
By Sarah Gertrude Millin
6s. net

IN *The Dark River* the authoress presents a deep and intimate study of life as it is lived in the diamond fields and cities of South Africa. Still more, it is a deep and penetrating study of those passions that rule the lives of men everywhere. Behind all, for local colour and setting, is the bare South African landscape.

THE BOOK OF YOUTH
By Margaret Skelton
7s. 6d. net

THIS novel by a new author reaches a very high level. It is a romantic story that begins in the country in somewhat idyllic vein, but later plunges into the broth of modern London life, coloured clearly by actual experience. The reader will find in it evidences of the new spirit of young minds struggling towards self-expression; but it is difficult to describe by such pedantic phrases a vivid and extremely readable novel that should make a wide appeal, not only to the younger generation.

THE DUCHESS OF SIONA
By Ernest Goodwin
Author of *The Caravan Man.* *7s. net*

MR GOODWIN made an undoubted success with his first novel. This novel, no less than the last, will find many readers, for it is, although the subject-matter is mighty different, instinct with the same qualities of fine sense, humour and pathos, On this occasion the author leaves modern life for the atmosphere of romance, the dusky alluring middle ages.

THE CASK
By Freeman Wills Crofts
7s. net

A SPLENDID mystery story, the ingenious handling of which leads to some of the most thrilling situations imaginable. Detective stories have a way of concealing essential facts from the reader, and ending in consequent flatness. No reader, we dare to predict, will find this fault in *The Cask* mystery. The story takes us to three great cities, London, Paris, and Glasgow, and is a thorough going, full of shudders, detective problem.

20th CENTURY FRENCH WRITERS
By Madame Duclaux
Illustrated from Photographs.   Extra Crown 8vo.   7s. 6d. net

THIS is not a book of biographical detail but a clever analysis of the brilliant band of 20th century French poets and novelists, who not only sang for the glory of France, but readily shed their blood for the love of it. Madame Duclaux is gifted with a facile pen, sparkling, witty, incisive, and the charm of a great literary reputation pervades the book. Some of those who are here described are:—Maurice Barrès, Romain Rolland, Edmond Rostand, Paul Claudel, Charles Péguy, Comtesse de Noailles.

SONGS from a YOUNG MAN'S LAND
By Sir Clive Phillipps-Wolley
Large Crown 8vo.   Cloth, 5s. net

SIR CLIVE PHILLIPPS-WOLLEY was a very remarkable Canadian. He was a pioneer of the Far West, a wonderful naturalist and had an intimate acquaintance with the Indian trappers and hunters. He did a great deal to further the commercial and industrial development of the Far West, but, above all, he was a pioneer of practical Imperialism. All of these qualities are reflected in his poems, while as a stylist he may be said to be a disciple or even a forerunner of Kipling.

THEODOR FONTANE: A Critical Study
By Kenneth Hayens, M.A.
Extra Crown 8vo.   7s. 6d. net

THIS is a short critical and biographical study of Theodor Fontane the German poet, journalist and novelist. Fontane was born in Brandenburg in 1819 and died in 1895. During his long life he passed through many phases. He was apprenticed chemist, made a precarious living by ballad writing and articles, came to London in the 'fifties as special correspondent and was war correspondent during the wars that led up to the foundation of the German Empire. In 1878 he published his great novel *Vor Dem Sturm.*

Collins' Spring List — 1920

Two New and Cheaper Editions

A WRITER'S RECOLLECTIONS
By Mrs Humphry Ward

Large Crown 8vo. With Two Photogravure Plates. 6s. net

THIS book, which had so wonderful a reception on its first appearance, is now put out in its *third edition*. In its delightful pages will be found many of the most interesting figures of the day—Gladstone, Morley, Balfour, Jowett, Pusey, Henry James, Pater, and a whole host of others.

'The panorama of a generation, the expression of an ideal, the quintessence of Victorianism in its best and fullest flower.' —*Daily Chronicle.*

'A perfect treasure house of good things, a gallery of speaking portraits. Few if any living writers can sketch a portrait so quickly, so incisively, so lovingly.'—*Evening Standard.*

PETROGRAD : The City of Trouble
By Meriel Buchanan
Daughter of the Former British Ambassador

With a Preface by Hugh Walpole. Crown 8vo. 3s. 6d. net

THIRD IMPRESSION

'The dominant impression left upon me is that the author is a sportswoman of the first order. You see her pressing to the windows to observe the shooting in the streets, going out to shop, to dine, to dance during the stormy months of the various phases of the Russian Revolutions . . . it hasn't a dull or insincere page.'—*Punch.*

Recent Publications 1919-1920

Some Books for the Library
IRISH IMPRESSIONS
By G. K. Chesterton
SECOND IMPRESSION. Crown 8vo. 7s. 6d. net

'A clever, witty, brilliant book which must have given him much pleasure.'—*Daily Chronicle*.

'Ought to be read by all Englishmen who care a fig for the honour of Englishmen.'—James Douglas in the *Star*.

'A genuine effort to understand what the Irish want and why they want it.'—Hamilton Fyfe in the *Daily Mail*.

'Without value.'—*Irish Times*.

'Irishmen will read the book with keen relish.'—*Irish Independent*.

A GARDEN OF PEACE
By F. Littlemore   10s. 6d. net
A Medley in Quietude
SECOND IMPRESSION. With many Illustrations. Demy 8vo.

'That delightful *olla podrida* which seems so easy to all great gardeners . . . there is just that *soupçon* of cayenne pepper in it that makes the whole most readable.'—*Evening Standard*.

'A charming volume, beautifully illustrated.'—*Daily News*.

AMONG ITALIAN PEASANTS
Written and Illustrated by Tony Cyriax
With an Introduction by MUIRHEAD BONE   12s. 6d. net
Six Illustrations in Colour and Ten in Black and White. Small 4to.

'The real life of Italy, as distinguished from the Italy of the tourist, is exceptionally well described. Her pictures . . . represent the simple Italian peasantry more faithfully perhaps than a more conventional art might do . . . not only entertaining in itself, but also throws much light on the domestic problems of Italy.'—*Spectator*.

'Most of all, it will delight lovers of Italy. There are no hackneyed descriptions of the Italy known to the ordinary traveller, or crude pictures in vivid colours such as we have almost learnt to expect of the portrayers of Italy's beauties . . . illustrations which show the bold simplicity of a master hand.'—*Country Life*.

Recent Publications   *1919-1920*

COUSIN PHILIP
By Mrs Humphry Ward
THIRD LARGE IMPRESSION.   7s. net

'Mrs Humphry Ward has renewed her own youth in studying the youth of these after-war days.'—*Daily Chronicle.*

'A novel which even the jaded reviewer reads with pleasure.'—*Saturday Review.*

'Mrs Ward cannot resist piling delicate agony upon delicate agony until we are brimful of anticipatory shudders.'—*Athenæum.*

MADELEINE
By Hope Mirrlees
SECOND IMPRESSION.   7s. net

'A first novel that deserves the warmest applause.'—*Morning Post.*

'Brilliant.'—*Nation.*

'There has been nothing so fine and true in its mode ... since John Inglesant.'—*Illustrated London News.*

'A remarkable first novel.'—*Manchester Guardian.*

'This difficult and interesting novel.'—*Times Literary Supplement.*

'Really promising.'—*Outlook.*

'Distinctly an achievement.'—*New Age.*

TRUE LOVE
By Allan Monkhouse
Author of *Men and Ghosts.*   7s. net

'Naked sincerity made articulate with preciseness and artistry.'—*Observer.*

'Strokes of spiritual illumination which lift Mr Monkhouse's novels into the rank of the elect.'—Edward Garnett in *Daily News.*

'An interesting and painfully engrossing story.'—*Spectator.*

Recent Publications　　　　1919-1920

Books by Francis Brett Young
MARCHING ON TANGA
With General Smuts in East Africa
A NEW EDITION.　　With Six Plates in Colour
Numerous Illustrations in Black and White; Map, etc.
Small Crown 4to.　10s. 6d. net

'The best written of all the books produced during the war by men on active service. Its imaginative quality and charm of its style were no surprise to those who knew his early novels.'—London Mercury.

POEMS: 1916-1918
Large Crown 8vo.　Boards.　5s. net

'Mr Brett Young is, in truth, if not one of the most nearly perfect, certainly one of the most interesting poets of to-day.'—New Statesman.

'It is unusual to find so much strength of thought, beauty of words, sincerity, imaginative vision, and technical accomplishment combined.'—Rose Macaulay in Daily News.

'Here, unless one is gravely mistaken, is something very like the real, imperishable thing.'—Manchester Guardian.

CAPTAIN SWING
A Romantic Play of 1830 in Four Acts
(Written in conjunction with W. Edward Stirling)
Crown 8vo.　Paper.　2s. net

THE YOUNG PHYSICIAN
SECOND IMPRESSION　7s. net

.'Giving us its author's best and placing him high indeed on the æsthetic plateau of performers in fiction.'—Thomas Seccombe in the Daily Chronicle.

'Lifted far above the average story in expression.'—Morning Post.

'One of the most vital stories ever written.'—Illustrated London News.

Recent Publications 1919-1920

THE PLAIN GIRL'S TALE
By H. H. Bashford
Author of *The Corner of Harley Street*, etc.
SECOND IMPRESSION.   7s. 6d. net

'A remarkably strong portrait, bold and intimate in feature.' —*Morning Post*.
'A happy book.'—*Times*.
'Able, interesting, and sincere to a degree by no means common.'—*Westminster Gazette*.
'She is adorable.'—W. L. George in *The World*.

FULL CIRCLE
By Mary Agnes Hamilton
Author of *Dead Yesterday*, etc..   7s. net

'Delightfully fresh, intensely arresting.'—*Scotsman*.
'An admirable portrait gallery.'—*Daily News*.

SIR LIMPIDUS
By Marmaduke Pickthall
Author of *Oriental Encounters*, etc..   7s. net

'Wonderfully unforced vein of irony.'—*Times*.
'The irony cuts like a whip-lash.'—*Express*.
'Really fun.'—*Observer*.

NEW WINE
By Agnes and Egerton Castle
SECOND IMPRESSION.   7s. net

'Mr and Mrs Egerton Castle are old hands at the game and can be relied on to tell a good story, and tell it well.'—*Daily Chronicle*.
'Not only very readable, but worth pondering over.'—*British Weekly*.

Recent Publications   1919-1920

THE HUMAN CIRCUS
By J. Mills Whitham
Author of *Fruit of the Earth*.   7s. net

'Has so great a gift of scenic suggestion that, with the minimum of effort, he produces a result that is almost decorative. The beaten child of the moor farm, the hills that run down to the sea, the gipsy camp, the travelling show, the London theatre: all these stand out with the sure carving of fine high relief.'—*Nation*.

OVER AND ABOVE
By J. E. Gurdon   7s. net

'The goodness of the book is based on certain rare and attractive features. Not only by airmen, but also by the laity, *Over and Above* will be read with more than ordinary interest.'—*Times*.

A Book for Boys

THE QUIETNESS OF DICK
By R. E. Vernède
Author of *Letters to My Wife*.   7s. net

'This posthumous work by the late Mr R. E. Vernède, who died of wounds in France in the middle of a successful literary career, has all the high spirits that characterised his writing . . . a rattling story of schoolboys in the holidays which will amuse the grown-ups who have been boys themselves.'—*Times Literary Supplement*.

'Mr R. E. Vernède, one of the chief literary losses of the war, left behind him a book for boys and men (which nowadays includes women) of excellent quality. Well written, high spirited, direct in incident, sly of humour . . . one of the best of its kind.'—*Morning Post*.